TO
LUC mou!

ENJOY
the
BOOK! —

with Best
Regads —

Dan

Praise for *Reimagining Industry Growth*

"Dan Varroney's *Reimagining Industry Growth* is a must-read for forward-looking executives who want to stay ahead of market trends and be able to better understand market moves. It is filled with insights, stories, and real-world, concrete examples of success in this fast-changing, volatile economic environment. Once you start reading, you won't be able to put it down. It's that good. I am recommending that my graduate students read it from cover to cover to better understand future business movements."

—Dr. David K. Rehr,
Professor and Director, Center for Business Civic Engagement,
Schar School of Policy and Government, George Mason University

"In a world of increasing complexity, Dan Varroney's insights and analytics are helping industries and trade associations push the envelope and identify the art of the possible. Challenging traditional thinking, Dan's customer-centric and partnership ideals are setting a new precedent for how trade association leaders and industry executives collaborate in support of sustainable value creation."

—Chris Astley,
Chairman, INDA (Nonwovens Industry Trade Association)

"Dan Varroney's career has prepared him to be an excellent advisor on the advantages trade associations can give their members. He is uniquely qualified by experience to write this helpful book."

—Newt Gingrich,
Former Speaker of the U.S. House of Representatives, bestselling author

"In *Reimagining Industry Growth*, Dan Varroney provides powerful insights for both industries and professions in these incredibly unpredictable times. Many sectors are struggling independently to prepare for the future, to protect and ensure their outcomes when facing uncertainty. Dan's intriguing propositions offer surprising revelations to achieve collaborative growth through strategic relationships with real-life case studies. He shows how any industry can benefit from effectively using trade associations to exponentially increase support, influence, and resiliency. Dan's methodology reveals the strategic advantages that we used at Finseca in designing our (communities-based) platform model, which I believe is the key to the reunification, agility, and continued evolution of our profession. Every CEO, executive, and board member could benefit from reading Dan's book."

—Kelly Kidwell,
Immediate Past Chair of Finseca, and CEO, Pacific Advisors

"In today's fast-paced and constantly evolving world, *Reimagining Industry Growth* by Dan Varroney provides practical guidance, actionable insights, and effective strategies to help industries and trade associations utilize the power of partnerships to drive success."

—Melissa Hockstad,
President and CEO, American Cleaning Institute

"Dan Varroney has placed his finger on the pulse of the importance of strategic partnerships in his new book, *Reimagining Industry Growth: Strategic Partnership Strategies in an Era of Uncertainty*. Association CEOs are servant leaders. As such, our primary job is to make certain that we are providing the highest level of service to our members while also giving the unvarnished advice and counsel needed to make critical choices for our industry. I hope you will enjoy Dan's book. I wish I had had this advice when I was beginning my career."

—Kevin M. Burke,
President and CEO, Airports Council International – North America (ACI-NA)

"In this book, Dan's wealth of experience with multiple industries and trade associations creates an essential read for both industry executives who are part of an association and association leaders themselves. Through a series of well-documented case studies, we are reminded of the inherent value for an industry in building strategic partnerships with their trade associations. Dan shares great insights on the purpose and importance of industry and trade association strategic partnerships, especially in a time of increasing uncertainty."

—Juan Carlos "JC" Scott
President and CEO, Pharmaceutical Care Management Association

"*Reimagining Industry Growth* is a powerful exploration of what is possible when businesses work together. Our economy is appropriately based on competition. But some challenges are too profound—and some opportunities too great—to be addressed by individual companies. Strategic partnerships create outcomes that are far greater than the sum of their parts. Dan Varroney explores exactly what goes into such partnerships and provides a roadmap for those trying to build something beyond what people currently imagine."

—David Chavern,
President and CEO, News Media Alliance

REIMAGINING
INDUSTRY
GROWTH

DANIEL A. VARRONEY

REIMAGINING
INDUSTRY
GROWTH

*Strategic Partnership
Strategies in an
Era of Uncertainty*

WILEY

Library of Congress Cataloging-in-Publication Data

Names: Varroney, Daniel A., author.
Title: Reimagining industry growth : strategic partnership strategies in an
    era of uncertainty / Daniel A. Varroney.
Description: Hoboken, New Jersey : John Wiley & Sons, Inc., [2022] |
    Includes bibliographical references and index.
Identifiers: LCCN 2021043984 (print) | LCCN 2021043985 (ebook) | ISBN
    9781119855927 (cloth) | ISBN 9781119855941 (adobe pdf) | ISBN
    9781119855934 (epub)
Subjects: LCSH: Strategic alliances (Business) | Strategic planning. |
    Industries. | Industrial management.
Classification: LCC HD69.S8 V37 2022 (print) | LCC HD69.S8 (ebook) | DDC
    658—dc23
LC record available at https://lccn.loc.gov/2021043984
LC ebook record available at https://lccn.loc.gov/2021043985

Cover Design: Wiley
Cover Image: © phochi/Shutterstock

SKY10030308_111821

For Jeanine, my wife, my princess, the light and love of my life

CONTENTS

FOREWORD

Dan Varroney is uniquely qualified to define the takeaway points explained in this book. His work experiences continuously gain him access to both industry association leaders and their member CEOs who are at the top of their game. From Dan's vantage point, he has watched, learned from, and now coaches association leaders on overcoming impediments, shaping the external environment, and assisting with the achievement of long-term growth for their industry.

Getting involved in our industry association, the National Marine Manufacturers Association (NMMA), is one of the smartest decisions I ever made. I can't take credit for it; I was invited to join by a respected board member. I entered the association thinking that I had signed up for another unpaid job, and that it would be a chore. Instead, I encountered the opportunity to meet and learn from the smartest people in our industry, which allowed our company to build relationships with the best, brightest, and most forward-thinking captains of our industry and their companies.

A natural outgrowth of these relationships is formal and informal strategic partnerships that propel our company. These are close working relationships with suppliers and customers that are essential to growing a successful business.

If you are charged with growing your business, this book proves that joining your industry association *and* committing yourself and your organization to actively supporting it will pay you back at least 10-fold. You will get smarter quicker, and you will meet the best people in the industry. The time and effort you commit will enable you to forge business-to-business partnerships with the best suppliers and customers. You will better understand where your competitors are going so that you can either challenge them or lead your company elsewhere with a higher probability for success. You can see into the future before it happens. Over time you can shape the industry in relatively simple and obvious ways to fuel growth for all players in the industry.

Industry associations have the unique ability to accomplish what their individual members cannot on their own. For example, they can pool the members' resources and promote the industry on a national scale, lifting demand for the industry's products and services. (A great example is the "Got Milk?" campaign, for which the dairy farmers in California paid three cents per gallon.) Similarly, associations can staff a team of people to represent the industry at the federal and state level to help shape the laws that will allow the industry to prosper. An association can make an effective case to regulators and legislators in ways that no member could ever achieve on their own. It takes industry participation and commitment to accomplish these things in a meaningful way.

Trade association executives will find a blueprint in this book for engaging their members and opening pathways to increase the value proposition of their association, which will, in turn, grow the membership and help make the association more successful and give it more clout to shape the environment in which the industry operates.

Steve Heese

President, Chris-Craft and

Chairperson, National Marine Manufacturers Association

INTRODUCTION

This book is a call to action for executives, companies, trade associations, and industries. We have experienced a great deal of volatility and change over the past two decades. That is nothing new in history. But what does seem to be new and maybe unique to this era is the speed at which everything is happening, and the immediacy of our awareness—if not necessarily our understanding—of it all.

In 2007–2008, the world's economy had a meltdown. The reasons are many and varied, and far beyond the scope of this book, but for a lot of people it was a wake-up call. Businesses across the globe in almost every industry were forced to reevaluate their strategic approach to over-the-horizon potentialities and had to begin learning to prepare in new and innovative ways for the unknown unknowns (or unk unks, as the engineering crowd would have it) that are now clearly a regular feature of the future landscape.

Many businesses rose to the challenge.

Despite uncertainty, companies still found themselves on the receiving end of record revenue and earnings performance. From 2009 to early 2020, the U.S. stock market reached historic highs, unemployment reached historic lows, and more Americans were working than ever before.

And then COVID-19 came crashing in. It spread fear, took many lives, caused shutdowns that eliminated millions of jobs and wages, and sent the international marketplace into a tailspin. It accelerated change and disrupted every business sector. Mike Tyson once said that everyone has a plan until they get punched in the face. COVID-19 packed quite a punch. And there were other challenges in 2020. It was a year for the history books.

The world is still reeling in many places and is at best unsteady in many others. But 2020 was not a knockout punch. In fact, by the end of that year, the Dow Jones had rallied and surpassed 30,000 for the first time, which had been as formidable and elusive a psychological barrier as the four-minute mile. Some see the hallmarks of another, even more dire, bubble. We shall see.

In the meantime, as we begin to rethink and reimagine the future, I would like to offer several propositions that I think are worth pondering—or at least considering—as you read on.

1. Black swans now apparently flock together.

2. People who see crisis and change as windows of opportunity adapt more easily than people who see unexpected difficulties as harbingers of doom.

3. Elections have consequences, and there are infrequent shifts in party control. Political partisanship and ideological divisions, while consequential (and at times unhealthy for the public weal), need not necessarily upend or derail economic progress and industry growth.

4. People who proactively pursue robust and durable personal relationships—whether in business, politics, clubs, or on the front porch—tend to be more resilient in hard times than others. Tight-knit communities fare better when threatened than individuals. As we will see in the stories ahead, harnessing vibrant communities is one of the keys to success in any arena.

Lifelong friendships and rich enduring marriages and relationships are the highest social expressions of our natural relational inclinations. Strategic partnerships are expressions of the same relational dynamic in business. Both are hard to get right, but when we do, they are among the most reliable and influential resources we have at our disposal. Because partnerships are an ideal expression of our nature, it seems common sense that we would pursue them in business. And more to the point, we should be pursuing them where they can be formed most naturally and in areas that are most likely to be mutually beneficial.

The most fertile ground, in my opinion, for nurturing strategic partnerships within any given industry is through trade associations. That assertion should be obvious to all industry leaders, but if widespread adoption is a fair indicator, the results are not there. It might be that people do not in fact see it or recognize the significant potential of the industry and trade association collaboration. Given the severe nature of today's challenges, it may seem too hard, or they would rather go it alone. Or it's something else. Or it's a mixture of all of the above. Regardless, the opportunity is there for the asking.

Forward-leaning trade associations have launched strategic partnerships with the industries they represent. For those that have, they provide some spectacular examples of what is possible when customer care and business prowess are combined with a relational mindset.

In the chaos of turbulent times, a solid partnership is an effective anchor and, in many cases, a safe harbor. And as we will see in Chapter 2, that kind of relationship is the reason that trade associations exist in the first place. And better still, partnership is one of the elements of our business planning that we can proactively choose and maintain a degree of control over.

Now is the time for a change in the way trade associations and the industries that they represent relate with one another, interact, and partner. It is the time for business executives to be focusing on developing, expanding, and solidifying strategic partnerships through the industry and trade associations that were designed for just such a purpose. It is time for trade associations to return to looking outward instead of inward.

This book provides actionable insights from the experiences of five trade association executives who purposely set out to represent their industries in such a way that all their members and everyone within their respective spheres of influence (or ecosystems, as they are styled) benefit and prosper. It also provides insights from the company leaders and captains of industry with whom they have partnered. In each case, the trade association reflects the values and desired outcomes of the industry they represent. In fact, each of these trade associations is widely regarded as the face of its respective industry. Their influence and efficacy are magnified by the synergy of their partnerships.

Corporate CEOs will discover new ways to think about and participate in their own trade association's value proposition. Business executives, academicians, elected and regulatory officials, undergraduate and graduate students, trade association leaders, and anyone interested in the practical value of forging lasting relationships will find examples of how it is done properly across a range of industries. The lessons are industry agnostic and fully transferable. I hope they will set the stage for a reassessment of current thinking and open the door to some unexplored and innovative ideas and approaches moving forward.

For trade association executives and their staff teams, this book provides a front row seat with industries and their leaders. It also conveys the effective utilization of the industry ecosystem, and it shares tangible examples of how trade associations and their strategic partnerships open pathways through these strategic partnerships. You will be able to utilize these examples as a baseline to build out strategic partnerships with your industry.

Chapter 1 examines the general nature and purpose of strategic partnerships, why they matter, and what makes them successful. We shall look at some of the more successful business-to-business partnerships and consider some of the characteristics that make them work. We shall uncover a few basic principles that are predictive of both effectiveness and durability in strategic partnerships, and we will consider some of the personal attributes of those who set out to make them happen and work hard to keep them strong.

Chapter 2 provides a short history of trade associations. We will look at why they exist in the first place, what they were created for, how they might have veered away from the original mission, and how customer-centricity and an outside-in way of thinking are returning these organizations to their original purpose.

Chapter 3 is about the great outdoors and how the recreational boating industry captures the allegiance of a growing list of consumers. A review of the industry reveals how an all-for-one focus throughout the supply chain extends the recreational boating industry's reach to the entire outdoor recreation ecosystem, not to mention impressive boat sales.

Chapter 4 looks at the baking industry, which has a long, storied, and meaningful history. It is built on a firm foundation of relationships. Through their trade association, the baking industry has propagated relationships that extend throughout a food and beverage ecosystem. The expanded relational foundation helps the industry manage its costs, innovate, and delight its consumers.

Chapter 5 investigates the unmanned systems community, its rapidly developing technologies, and its hope for a new, different, and possibly better world for us all. As with any truly disruptive technology, the industry has a chasm to cross. Their dominant trade association is working hard to achieve widespread public acceptance of autonomous vehicles by building a web of relationships across a vast community of natural market evangelists.

Chapter 6 sheds light on the asphalt pavement industry, which could be described as a community of data-driven engineers dedicated to doing good for everyone. From sustainability to safety to highway design, their trade association is where and how new research and development takes place. It is also a destination location where the industry connects, learns from one another, and seeks ways to continuously improve our quality of life through local, regional, and national road and highway systems that traverse and connect America.

Chapter 7 discusses the frozen foods industry, which is growing into a significant provider of food for our nation. Offering a wide array of healthy choices and consumer tastes, the industry is focused on becoming the number-one food packaging and delivery choice for food service businesses and consumers alike.

Chapter 8 assesses what has been learned and shares breakthrough opportunities for industries and trade associations. Since the next "punch in the face" is likely to be right around the corner, this book is a call to action. It is time to embrace change. It is time to bring to bear all our best tools for navigating new and sometimes frightening realities. It is time to learn lessons from the great models of cooperation and synergy. It is time to discover and utilize the roadmap for building and maintaining powerful coalitions and alliances.

This book is about how industry leaders absorb blows, learn valuable lessons, and then reimagine industry growth.

1 Strategic Partnerships

Persistent Hard Times: The Mother of Strategic Partnerships

Just as necessity is the mother of invention, hard times may be the mother of strategic partnerships. Turbulent and uncertain times have always inspired people to search for new and innovative ways to endure and to triumph. Ordinary people sometimes rise to greatness in a crisis. We are capable of overcoming adversity and achieving lofty and heroic breakthroughs during moments of intense challenge. Some great business partnerships were created to weather tough times; sometimes those tough times are due to internal issues, sometimes external issues, sometimes uncontrollable circumstances, sometimes extraordinary opportunities, and occasionally in preparation to achieve the next breakthrough.

Defining Strategic Partnerships

It must be said up front that a strategic partnership does not guarantee success. Successful partnerships are not a given. In fact, a good and lasting strategic partnership is not unlike a good and lasting marriage. It requires shared vision, shared values, clear and honest communication, perseverance, and perhaps more than anything, commitment—unswerving commitment that breaks through the most difficult barriers. It is hard work.

It must also be said that strategic partnerships come in all shapes and sizes and textures and colors and flavors. Although there are general rules and organizing principles that provide the context and outlines, each one is—also like a marriage or long-term relationship—unique.

The generic term *strategic partnership* entered the business lexicon many years ago, and much has been written on the subject. Today, business analysts and consultants speak of strategic branding partnerships, strategic supply chain partnerships, strategic research and development partnerships, strategic finance partnerships, strategic human resources partnerships, and so on. Successful strategic partnerships have been highly effective in countering the negative forces of market volatility, particularly through the last several decades.

Wall Street's insistence on perpetual growth has sometimes been criticized as impractical, short-sighted, and greed-driven. But it has also spurred creativity and newly minted out-of-the-box thinking, and it has produced cooperation in unexpected places.

Most of the writing on strategic partnerships focuses on how companies have combined their strengths and mitigated their weaknesses to expand customer bases, brand recognition, marketing opportunities, and market reach to increase productivity, to broaden investment opportunity and sustainability, and ultimately to grow revenue and profitability for the participating companies. We shall be looking at an even more prodigious, inclusive, and ambitious type of strategic partnership—the sort that moves the needle for entire industries.

But first let's consider several of the widely hailed strategic partnerships so that we're on the same page regarding what we mean by the term, and then we shall explore the power of strategic partnerships through the lens of five industry trade associations.

Some Successful Strategic Partnerships

In 1993, Barnes & Noble teamed up with Starbucks Coffee "to provide a consistent, quality cup of coffee for readers to enjoy while perusing the latest best-sellers."[1] Today, nearly every Barnes & Noble bookstore has a Starbucks café either conjoined or inside the store. The partnership has been a boon not only to both companies' retail operations, but also to the pleasure of their shared customers. And while it may be a case of correlation rather than causation, it is interesting to note that Barnes & Noble is the last big box chain bookstore standing.

In 1994, Starbucks and PepsiCo joined forces to create the North American Coffee Partnership (NACP). Two years later they launched the now iconic bottled Frappuccino, and with it the ready-to-drink (RTD) coffee category in the beverage industry. Over the past 25 years, the combination of Starbucks' coffee expertise with PepsiCo's vast sales and distribution network has both expanded and dominated the RTD coffee and energy drink sectors. NACP continues to innovate and grow. By 2016 it was a $2-billion-plus retail business in its own right.[2]

In 2015, Starbucks and Spotify began a collaboration that gives baristas and customers more say over local café music playlists, provides continuous access to music streaming through both Starbucks and Spotify apps, and allows premium Spotify members to earn Starbuck's rewards points. This strategic partnership was formed in response to rapidly changing music culture and preferences and the technological advances that seem to be driving them. Sharing customers has helped keep both brands not only relevant but on the cutting edge of customer satisfaction.

The keen observer will note that all three examples just mentioned involve Starbucks. This is not to intentionally promote Starbucks (which is one of the top 50 most valuable brands on the planet[3]), but to highlight a critical factor that is, deliberately, at the core of Starbucks' meteoric rise and sustained growth: relationships. The value of genuine relationship orientation (both internal and external) in trailblazing through uncertain times, as we shall see, cannot be overstated. In the spirit of transparency, I was and continue to be personally greatly influenced by former Starbucks CEO Howard Schultz's *Pour Your Heart Into It*.[4]

There have been many fruitful and well-regarded strategic partnerships over the years. Consider, for example, Hewlett-Packard and Disney, Renault and Nissan, Apple and Nike (Nike+), Ford and Eddie Bauer, BMW and Montblanc, and many others that have likewise served the partnering companies (and their customers) well. A fair number of these partnerships (though sadly not most) have stood the test of time. There are only a few, however, that have actually transformed entire industries. These will be our focus. But first we must explore some of the guiding principles, values, and traits that characterize the most successful strategic partnerships and the leaders who forge them.

Some Defining Characteristics of Successful Strategic Partnerships and Their Creators

There are three primary intertwined passions that fuel the most successful CEOs, boards, and the strategic partnerships they create (see Figure 1.1):

1. Customer-centricity
2. Relationship-centricity
3. Business-centricity

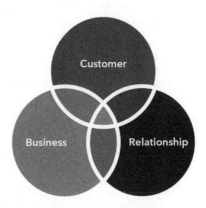

Figure 1.1 The Makings of a Strategic Partnership
Source: Illustration artwork prepared by Erin Wagner, Edge Research.

The nexus of these three powerful driving forces is where great leaders and lasting partnerships reside, both in good times and bad. In trying times—times of change, challenge, and uncertainty—there is little hope for survival outside the confluence of customer-, relationship-, and business-centricity. The customer is preeminent for the simple reason that without a happy customer base, there is no business. So, let us start with the customer.

Customer Preeminence

The outside-in approach allows executives to see their company in its proper relation to the bigger picture. It starts with the perspective of the customer, the client, the end user. It seeks to thoroughly understand their needs, problems, hopes, and dreams. It seeks to overthrow assumptions and received wisdom and myths about what the customer wants and replace them with clear understanding and certain knowledge and truth about what the customer wants. This can often be achieved by systematically collecting and analyzing qualitative and quantitative research supplemented by simply listening to and internalizing customer feedback.

Another way of knowing what the customer wants is to understand what P.G. Wodehouse's inimitable Bertie Wooster referred to as "the psychology of the individual," to understand the customer by understanding human nature.

Here again, Howard Schultz is my model for implementation of the outside-in concept. His thinking is captured perfectly by Matthew Dollinger in a *Fast Company* interview with a Starbucks manager named Kelly: "Starbucks' goal is to become the Third Place in our daily lives . . . 'We want to provide all the comforts of your home and office. You can sit in a nice chair, talk on your phone, look out the window, surf the web . . . oh, and drink coffee too.'" Dollinger was astonished by that final detail: "(Notice she put "drink coffee" last???).["5] That puts the idea quite neatly in a nutshell. The focus is not first on what we can offer, but on what the customer needs and wants.

Sometimes the outside-in approach is counterintuitive from a traditional sales perspective. If, for example, my particular capabilities do not match up with a prospective customer's immediate wants and needs, our initial relationship might be built by my seeking to guide them to the people who can in fact meet their current needs. Again, the outside-in approach regards every relationship first through the eyes of the customer rather than from the perspective of an organization's own products and services.

The outside-in frame of reference is critical to success in a topsy-turvy world in which everyone has access to a veritable smorgasbord of information and quite literally a whole world of choices. The age of "build it and they will come" has passed.

The inside-out frame of reference, by contrast, is defined by a company's own products, services, strengths, and capabilities. It requires convincing the customer to see and understand and accept the company's point of view, rather than the other way around. Customers today are informed, sophisticated, and fickle. The survival of inward-looking companies depends on the few people who claim to "know" it (that is to say, "like" it—the company's products or services) when they see it," rather than on the masses who want what they want when and how they want it. The pool of the former is small, especially in comparison to the ocean of the latter.

It's a choice really between pleasing shareholders short-term (inside-out) or customers long-term (outside-in).

Sometimes companies try to sit on the fence: to have their cake and eat it. It's hard to do.

John Pepper, the former chairman and CEO of Procter & Gamble (P&G), once said: "At P&G the [first] stakeholders clearly were our consumers. They're the people we serve. If we're not serving well, we're not gonna have a business. Period."[6] That pretty well sums up *why* it all starts with the customer. But what of the *how*? How, practically, does a company make the customer preeminent? The approach I would suggest, and to which I have alluded, is known as outside-in thinking.

Jim Collins tells a story that beautifully illustrates the outside-in approach. In 1979, James Burke, CEO of Johnson & Johnson Co., was apparently concerned that the company was drifting away from its core values and especially its focus on the customer. He called a meeting of his top executives and startled them by smacking a copy of the J&J credo (written almost four decades earlier by R.W. Johnson, Jr.) and saying, "Here's the credo. If we're not going to live by it, let's tear it off the wall."[7]

One of the guiding principles that was of particular concern to Burke was a higher duty to "mothers and all others who use our products." That day Johnson & Johnson executives recommitted to the credo. When a crisis involving cyanide-poisoning of Tylenol came in 1982, there was no "need to debate whether customer safety outweighed short-term financial concerns, because the debating was already done."[8]

As a final note on customer-centricity, I would like to foreshadow some thoughts that we shall explore later in the context of strategic trade association partnerships: that is, the idea of the customer as a partner and the preeminence of the customer's customer.

Relationship Supremacy

There is no substitute for strong human relationships in navigating difficult circumstances. The power of two or three together is proverbial in many cultures for a reason. As King Solomon pointed out, "two are better than one because they have a good return for their labor; for if either of them falls, the one will lift up his companion."[9] It is an old, cross-cultural truth that neither a cord of three strands nor a bundle of twigs is easily broken.

Alliances are essential in building business solutions. According to a study done by Booz Allen Hamilton and the Kellogg School of Management (Northwestern University) in 2001, "Winning companies define and deploy relationships in a consistent, specific, multi-faceted manner . . . top-performing companies focus extraordinary, enterprise-wide energy on moving beyond a transactional mind-set as they develop trust-based, mutually beneficial, and long-term associations, specifically with four key constituencies: customers, suppliers, alliance partners, and their own employees."[10]

John Pepper had a slightly different take on the key constituencies, but the principle that relationships matter holds firm. For him the P&G stakeholders were, in order of importance, customers first (for the reason stated earlier); then the employees, who must be enabled to flourish; then the stockholders and the financial analysts who report on the stock; and finally, the community at large. "Who are the stakeholders? That's a blunt mechanical term, but what it's really saying is: who are the people to whom we owe service? and who by serving, we can succeed."[11]

Human relationships are at the core of every partnership, whether personal, economic, or political; whether between individuals, corporations, or nations. And strong human relationships are vital to any successful endeavor. Different kinds of relationships and partnerships may require different strengths and different focal points, but the underlying characteristics of successful relationships are always present.

Before we go on, let us be clear that by successful I mean to say *mutually beneficial.* Both (or all) parties must prosper and achieve desirable outcomes. One need not look very far to find partnerships, or alliances, or even friendships that dissolve or collapse or are destroyed by lies, broken commitments, betrayals, and so forth. We are not here seeking to solve the great mysteries of human meaning and motivation, but we must at least acknowledge that there are pitfalls that can perhaps be mitigated if not avoided altogether.

There is much disagreement about how best to relate to people. Machiavelli mistakenly thought fear a better motivator than love. Some adhere to a golden rule variant that says he who has the gold rules. This is also a mistake. Jesus upended the old eye-for-an-eye prescription with the actual Golden Rule: Do unto others as you would have them do to you. This last, in my experience, works best in human relations and strategic partnerships. And it passes the reasonable person test. Truth is more productive for relationships than lies. Transparency is better than deceit. Freedom is preferable to bondage. Love is far more desirable than fear. For most people, these are the principles that work best in durable long-term relationships.

For all the piles of books on the subject, there really are just a few basic guidelines that tend toward creating and maintaining stable long-term relationships generally, and successful strategic partnerships particularly. These are:

- Alignment on values and outcomes
- Honest communication and transparency
- Commitment and trust

Alignment on Values and Outcomes

Lasting relationships depend upon solid and committed agreement both on the destination and on the rules for getting there. Some questions must be settled up front or they will tear relationships apart:

- What are we willing to give up in exchange for success?
- Are we willing to compromise? (And if so, what are we willing to compromise?)
- Are we open to detours, or even changing destinations?

Oxen unequally yoked together is the best analogy I can think of to illustrate the point. It is admittedly a bit old-fashioned, but it is apt. If you have ever tried to plow a field with oxen, you will know that if the stronger tries to pull the weaker in a straight line, both will eventually collapse from exhaustion; if they go at their own pace without fighting each other, they will plow in circles. Successful relationships depend on an equal yoke—shared values and outcomes.

Honest Communication and Transparency

For strategic partnerships to have any hope of surviving over time, all participants must be absolutely committed to continual, truthful communication and thoroughgoing transparency regarding not only opportunities, strengths, and aspirations, but also risks, weaknesses, potential threats, and all the other subjects about which polite society would prefer never to speak.

In a 2014 study, the Business Performance Innovation (BPI) Network and the Chief Marketing Officer (CMO) Council found that more than half of respondents reported a high failure rate (more than 60 percent) of strategic partnerships. One of the reasons for the high failure rate is the simple fact that "strategic partnerships need a level of transparency, integration and communication that is quite frankly, quite frightening. You have to expose yourself to the other party, you have to understand their businesses. Maybe you have to share your risks and concerns, and listen [to theirs]."[12]

Honest, transparent communication is difficult at the best of times in the best of relationships. Throw in money as a motivator, and perhaps even survival as an entity, and it becomes that much harder. But to ignore it is to fail.

Commitment and Trust

It probably goes without saying that for relationships to last, trust must be high (and scrupulously maintained), and each party must be absolutely committed to the success of the partnership and to the success of each of the parties. Unwavering commitment is one of the touchstones of every mutually beneficial relationship. When commitment falters, or is even perceived to falter, trust fails and partnerships unravel. Strong commitment in the face of all obstacles builds not only trust, but the perseverance and endurance necessary to prevail over all fear and uncertainty. There is no substitute for commitment and trust.

Business Dominance

While no strategic partnership (or any business endeavor, for that matter) can succeed over time without a strong focus on the customer first and then on *all* (internal and external) relationships of consequence, neither can they succeed without superior business thinking and engagement.

There are those who might regard customer care and relational talent as "soft" capabilities. Soft capabilities can, to some degree, be faked. One can pay lip service to caring for customers and adopt an ersatz care for employees, partners, stakeholders, and whoever else (though no fraud can be perpetrated indefinitely). The truth will surface, but not always quickly.

By contrast, it is impossible to fake business prowess in turbulent times for very long. There are far too many highly capable and highly motivated competitors. The business piece of the Venn diagram is not optional. Successful strategic partnerships must understand the business environment in which they operate, and they must act brilliantly and decisively to carry the day.

My research and my own experience justify the choice of five characteristics of CEOs, boards, and the strategic partnerships they create that are leading indicators of success:

1. Strategic thinking
2. Business acumen
3. Focus on data and analytics
4. Defined outcomes, effectiveness measures, and key performance indicators (KPIs)
5. Constructive governance, leadership, and processes

Note: I am not trying to teach anything new or surprising here. This is all well-plowed ground. I am simply aiming to draw your attention to the aspects of these success indicators that seem to play a particularly important role in strategic partnerships that are proactively getting out in front to lead during times of adversity.

Strategic Thinking

The relatively recent inclusion of scenario planning as a key ingredient in the strategic planning process is indispensable. If you want to reimagine growth in unpredictable times, you need to learn to account for the unknown unknowns. Scenario planning seeks to get every possible outcome, imaginable and unimaginable, on the table. The unimaginable may be represented only as x possibility, but it cannot be ignored. As J.R.R. Tolkien put it in *The Hobbit*, "It does not do to leave a live dragon out of your calculations, if you live near him."

The planning process ranks possible occurrences and outcomes by their likelihood of happening and by the potentially catastrophic consequences of ignoring them as possibilities, and then planning proceeds based on priorities and probabilities. Many generals throughout the ages would attest to the accuracy of General Eisenhower's assessment: "Plans are worthless, but planning is everything."[13] Eisenhower pointed out that the very nature of an emergency is that it is something that emerges unexpectedly and that it will not therefore happen according to your plan.

Business Acumen

Business acumen is a critical skill set for navigating the unexpected. I think of business acumen as having developed a sharp enough mind to allow you to quickly and accurately assess how things impact your business, your partner's business, and your competitor's business, and to act decisively (and correctly) in response to any market movements or changes, expected or unexpected. Others, as we shall see, have different definitions that are equally valid.

My friend Thom Dammrich, whom you will meet in Chapter 3, agrees that with association executives, "There's always a little bit of a gap on the business acumen. It's not just business acumen about the association, it's knowing the business fundamentals of the industry you serve and knowing how to convert that into making and saving them money."[14]

Focus on Data and Analytics

Sound business decisions and strategy planning rely heavily on ample and accurate data, and correct interpretation of its meaning. In May 2020, GoodData (a global analytics company) announced a new strategic partnership with Visa, Inc. (the credit card company) to "help companies of any size to become data companies."[15] A Visa spokesperson noted that "there's no better time to invest in areas that will improve the lives of consumers and businesses" than right now, in the midst of extreme, worldwide challenges. "With insights from data," she went on to say, "we can help sellers, financial institutions and Visa's extended global business network better understand and meet consumer needs, especially when those needs are changing fast."[16]

Defined Outcomes, Effectiveness Measures, and Key Performance Indicators (KPIs)

Many strategic partnerships that succeed take the time up front to work out a clear and unequivocal definition of what success looks like.

As with any business, a strategic partnership is enhanced by a set of metrics that are predictive of success. And these metrics, or KPIs, must be quantifiable and easily digestible.

One of the mistakes I have seen is the adoption of metrics used by one or the other of the participating companies or some sort of dashboard fusion. It rarely works. The partnership exists separate and distinct from the participating companies and will have its own definition of success and criteria for measuring that success. Time must be taken to think through the most desirable outcomes and what set of metrics is most predictive of those outcomes.

Another common and often fatal mistake I have seen is a poor balance between efficiency and effectiveness measurements on the dashboard. Efficiency measurements are lagging indicators; they measure activity. Activity is not usually predictive of anything at all because it becomes an end in itself. Effectiveness measurements are leading indicators because they measure customer behavior and outcomes. And good customer outcomes are predictive of success.

Constructive Governance, Leadership, and Processes

Although it should be obvious and intuitive, it needs to be said: Agreement on governance, leadership, and processes should be reached at the outset of a strategic partnership, not after things start to go sideways. Rules of engagement matter. Who makes decisions? And by what process and authority are decisions made? Who answers to whom? And about what? These kinds of simple questions should not be taken for granted. It is best to spell out functional duties and agree to them at the beginning. It does not pay to operate on assumptions.

These last two leading indicators of successful strategic partnerships (*defined outcomes, effectiveness measures, and KPIs* and *constructive governance, leadership, and processes*) are far more important in a business-to-business arrangement than in the context of industry partnerships with their own trade associations, for reasons that will become clear in the next chapter. Nevertheless, they are critical to formal partnerships and therefore worth including in the list. Trade association partnerships with their own members, and even within their own larger ecosystems, can be far less formal when the association is accepted as an extension of—or better yet, as the face of—the industry they represent.

A Few Defining Attributes of Successful CEOs and Successful Association Executives

There are many personality and character traits that can make for successful business leaders and successful partnerships. That is a subject well beyond the reach of this book. But the professionals and executives I have personally observed successfully navigating difficult and unexpected circumstances, chiefly in the context of trade association leadership, tend to share some attributes of character, personality, and style. These attributes, as we will see in the industry studies, are essential ingredients in the strategic partnerships between industries and their trade associations. It therefore seems fitting for me to share my own compendium of what I call success factors in trade association leadership:

- *Grand personality.* Many of the people I know and have observed leading industries through turbulent times thrive on helping a community of people succeed. They have sound judgment, are able to stay flexible, are passionately curious, and are comfortable with being uncomfortable. They are sometimes a bit larger than life.

- *Strategic collaboration.* Leaders engage all stakeholders before moving forward. They are both conveners and connectors, able to motivate boards, and able to negotiate strategic linkages (both acquisitions and partnerships).

- *Promotion.* They play offense, identify trends, and build solutions. Most of them serve as excellent external advocates in media outlets.

- *Data-driven insight.* Many care deeply about facts. They tend to see patterns that others miss. They harvest, synthesize, apply, and deploy data to adjust strategies and bring the marketplace together and brainstorm solutions.

- *Determination to deliver results.* Most are highly motivated to achieve good outcomes for themselves and—more importantly—for their partners. They are generous of spirit and devoted to the principle of self-interest properly understood (that is, what is good for the community is good for me).[17]

- *Informed bias for action.* Leaders seek innovative opportunities that outweigh risks. They are transparent but don't move too quickly because they must remain a neutral broker with a foot in both camps.

Businesses are finding that to keep up with the unprecedented pace of change and uncertainty that defines the marketplace today, they must approach over-the-horizon challenges the way the military has for some time now. That is, by employing scenario planning as a staple of their strategic planning approach and proactively seeking both exaptive and adaptive contingency responses.

Business in the modern global economy is not for the faint of heart; neither, it turns out, can it be easily done alone. No corporation is an island.

Before we go on, I need to be perfectly clearly on a couple of points. I described earlier a number of characteristics and attributes that are common to many of the strategic partnerships that I have studied in detail and that work. I also described some of the prominent personality and character traits of the people—mostly CEOs—who have forged strategic partnerships (many of whom I have known personally) that work. But please understand that I am not in any way suggesting that any single individual or any company needs to have all (or even most) of the attributes, characteristics, or personality traits that I have described. I am not saying that all you have to be is some lovely mixture of Mother Teresa and Superman in order to do this well.

The passion to serve customers, build and maintain relationships, and understand business is a universal predictor of success in strategic partnerships. And I do believe all three are necessary for a strategic partnership to succeed over time. But it must be noted that all three of those passions are actually a choice that can be made, and more importantly, a choice that can be made by almost anyone, with almost any degree of natural talent. Individuals and the companies they run get to decide what to focus their attention on. I am merely suggesting that strong partnerships depend more than anything else on choosing to focus on these three pillars.

I will grant that some people are better suited to one or another and are more naturally attuned to one or another of these pillars. Some people are blessed with a natural business savvy, or a head for numbers, or an inscrutable charisma, or a desire to serve. Others may have less intrinsic talent but a strong will to achieve. Still others may just recognize goodness when they see it. The recipe for success lies in understanding and honing your natural traits and talents, and compensating for the ones that you do not possess by building relationships with people who will fill in the gaps, if you will. Good leaders will choose staff, board members, and partners whose innate gifts and talents will help to round out the picture.

As a final step in preparing to present the case for leveraging trade associations to expand the use of strategic partnerships to help mitigate risk and uncertainty and position industries for growth in the face of massive disruption and adversity, let us now take a brief look at why trade associations exist in the first place and how they might better position themselves to help the communities they represent reimagine industry growth.

2 Trade Associations

Trade Associations *Are* Strategic Partnerships

It seems clear that strategic partnerships of all varieties are increasingly necessary and desirable in the modern global economy. This important factor is not apparently clear to most industry executives. It is one particular venue where strategic partnerships are vastly superior, both quantitatively and qualitatively, to all others, yet they are underutilized. And for every imaginable industry, that venue is already in place, and in a huge number of cases it has been for a very long time. The history of trade associations is instructive.

Collegia

"*Collegia* are thought to have existed since the beginning of the [Roman] Republic and were constituted of groups of individuals of similar interest, usually members who shared the same craft or trade."[1] Later, under the empire, one of the distinguishing marks of the *collegia* was that they provided "necessary work for public use."[2] Many of them were recognized and to some extent protected by the government because they provided a public service; their products or services were needed for the general good of society. The most prominent of the *collegia* that were authorized during the empire include textile dealers,[3] millers and bakers,[4] firefighters, builders, and carpenters.[5]

Notably, as we shall see later, bakers were among the first to be certified as essential workers during the COVID-19 pandemic in the United States. Firefighters, as first responders, fall into that category by default.

Guilds

The guilds of medieval Europe, including England, began to appear around a thousand years ago. There were two primary types: merchant guilds and craft guilds.[6] Early merchants traded their goods, which required travel. They banded together for mutual protection from thieves and other physical dangers inherent in travel on the highways and byways and high seas. Over time, as they prospered, merchants were able to hire others to do what was still the dangerous and often tedious work of trading goods, and the merchants themselves settled in cities and together flexed their newly discovered political influence to protect and grow their trade.

Bakers, weavers, stonemasons, goldsmiths, brewers, and anyone else who practiced a specialized craft formed craftsmen's guilds, mainly to protect the quality of their crafts and to ensure acceptable prices. The craft guilds were protectionist and exclusive by design. Membership in most of the craft guilds became a hereditary right, and usually heredity was a requirement. From a social standpoint, going into the family business was regarded as a responsibility.

Trade Associations

The *Encyclopedia Britannica* defines a trade association as a "voluntary association of business firms organized on a geographic or industrial basis to promote and develop commercial and industrial opportunities within its sphere of operation, to voice publicly the views of members on matters of common interest, or in some cases to exercise some measure of control over prices, output, and channels of distribution."[7]

One of the earliest associations in the United States that I'm aware of is The Carpenters' Company of the City and County of Philadelphia, which was founded in 1724.[8] The name is somewhat misleading because the members were not carpenters, per se (although most were skilled craftsmen), but rather were recognized as—and referred to themselves as—"Master Builders," who in the early days had the combined skills of architects, construction supervisors, and engineers.[9] The term *company* is the Old English word for association. Nevertheless, it was a trade association very much like what we would recognize as one today. And it still exists.

The Principle of Association

By the time the brilliant, perceptive, and prescient French political philosopher and commentator Alexis de Tocqueville arrived in 1831 to spend a year travelling, studying, and analyzing democracy in America, associations of every sort had sprung up all over the young nation. Tocqueville was quite taken by the phenomenon. "Americans of all ages, all conditions, and all dispositions, constantly form associations."[10] It intrigued him. "Wherever, at the head of some new undertaking, you see the government in France, or a man of rank in England, in the United States you will be sure to find an association. I met with several kinds of associations in America, of which I confess I had no previous notion; and I have often admired the extreme skill with which the inhabitants of the United States succeed in proposing a common object to the exertions of a great many men, and in getting them voluntarily to pursue it."[11]

For Tocqueville, the American habit of forming associations to accomplish common goals was truly extraordinary. He describes America as a country in which "men have in our time carried to the highest perfection the art of pursuing in common the object of their common desires."[12] And inescapable. "Amongst the laws which rule human societies there is one which seems to be more precise and clear than all others. If men are to remain civilized, or to become so, the art of associating together must grow and improve in the same ratio in which the equality of conditions is increased.[13]

He studied the issue with care and concluded that for Americans, in the context of a democratic experiment, associating together, pooling resources, and working for the common good was not so much a moral or idealistic impulse but a pragmatic response to the harsh reality that the survival of society depended on it.[14] The same is true for industries.

Business Leagues

Over the course of the century following de Tocqueville's astute observations regarding the American propensity for associating together for good reasons, trade associations were fruitful and multiplied. And by the time the Internal Revenue Service (IRS) was created in 1913 after the 16th Amendment to the U.S. Constitution was ratified, trade associations were an important and permanent feature of the business landscape.

Section 501(c)(6) of the Internal Revenue Code calls them business leagues and defines them thus:

An association of persons having some common business interest, the purpose of which is to promote such common interest and not to engage in a regular business of a kind ordinarily carried on for profit. Trade associations and professional associations are business leagues. To be exempt, a business league's activities must be devoted to improving business conditions of one or more lines of business as distinguished from performing particular services for individual persons. No part of a business league's net earnings may inure to the benefit of any private shareholder or individual and it may not be organized for profit to engage in an activity ordinarily carried on for profit (even if the business is operated on a cooperative basis or produces only enough income to be self-sustaining). The term *line of business* generally refers either to an entire industry or to all components of an industry within a geographic area.[15]

The phrases "devoted to improving business conditions" and "promote such common interest" are the salient points here. Business leagues, or trade associations, were formed to enable lines of business (that is, industries) to act together on behalf of entire industries. In other words, business leagues are strategic partnerships—but on a grand scale—industry-wide.

Fast-Forward to Now

The availability of these partnership opportunities for industries is growing. In 2020 alone, there were 62,480 business leagues (trade and professional organizations) in the United States recognized by the IRS.[16] Let that sink in for a moment. As far as I can tell, that means that just about every company in America has access to what could potentially be the perfect strategic partnership already in place. The question it begs, of course, is: Why isn't there greater acceptance?

The reason, I offer, is because the opportunities are either not recognized or not sufficiently understood. And even when they are, the human factor enters the picture. Competing interests and competing agendas can obscure the simple, overriding fact that working together is almost always better than working at odds, or at loggerheads, as some people used to say. Although trade associations were developed specifically to expand the reach of and leverage the collective power inherent in larger groups, too many have tended over time to buy into the Wall Street continuous-growth mantra. The magnitude of the missed opportunity is far more visible after you read the case studies.

Trade organizations are more ready than ever to help their industries overcome challenges and build consequential partnerships. Since the start of COVID-19, they are migrating rapidly from an inward-looking posture to an outward-looking focus. In multiple cases, trade associations are far more focused on how they can aid their members in moving the needle for the entire industry.

A recent example of a leading outward-looking association comes from the Global Business Alliance (GBA), a Washington, DC-based trade association that represents 200 of the largest international companies that operate in the United States. GBA president and CEO Nancy McLernon and her team established a wholly owned subsidiary, GBA Sentinel. The new product managed through the subsidiary, according to Ms. McLernon, "will give global companies access to the cutting-edge tools they need to efficiently audit and monitor their supply chains and digital assets. We believe this initiative will help rapidly advance our nation's effort to prevent future attacks and underscores how seriously world-class companies take protecting America's supply chains."[17]

This is one of numerous examples of how modern trade associations are strategic partners helping to move the needle. Trade associations like the GBA that adopt an outside-in rather the typical inside-out approach invariably prosper. There are many other examples such as the Airports Council–North America led by Kevin Burke, president and CEO. Before, during, and after the pandemic, Mr. Burke and his team have driven strategic partnerships to new levels. Because member-centricity is outside-in, achieving the necessary Cares Act funding, which kept airports solvent—a vital resource in shaping regulations—and provided vital virtual online training for professionals, airports valued their trade association's rapid response.

A New(ish) Word

There are increasingly more examples of the power of these partnerships. Some of this traction is based on new and challenging realities. In other words, it is difficult and expensive for a company to go it alone any longer. The neologism "coopetition" (meaning "cooperating with a competitor to achieve a common goal or get ahead"[18]) was invented to deal with exactly this problem. When we are seeking the same outcome, game theory is clear; we are better off working together than apart. Businesses have learned that lesson, one-on-one, and have discovered ways of cooperating while competing. Consider, as examples, "Apple and Samsung, DHL and UPS, Ford and GM, and Google and Yahoo."[19]

Imagine how much more effective it must be when the bulk of the companies within an entire industry are convened, and together their individual strengths are leveraged and their weaknesses covered under the artful watch of an industry champion that can remain independent, unbiased, and unencumbered by the need to make a profit: one whose sole interest and purpose is to achieve the best possible outcomes for the industry as a whole.

The fact is that a trade association exists precisely to be a strategic partner to the industry it represents. That is its raison d'être. Consider these ideas we shall explore briefly:

- In the United States, trade associations exist to help members promote one another's and the public good. This is proven by (1) the government's definition of a business league, and (2) the government's decision to grant a business league tax-exempt status in recognition of its inherent advantage to society.

- The same value proposition was understood by Imperial Rome (and the Republic before it).

- It was understood and reinstituted by the medieval guilds.

- And it emerges naturally and unfettered from the American character and from the American devotion to the principle of self-interest properly understood. "The Americans . . . are fond of explaining almost all the actions of their lives by the principle of interest rightly understood; they show with complacency how an enlightened regard for themselves constantly prompts them to assist each other . . ."[20]

A trade association is by its very essence a strategic partnership.

The good news is that successful strategic partnerships are individual-, company-, and industry-agnostic. And any board, CEO, and staff of any corporation or any trade or association in any industry can make a positive decision to adopt these principles and create a long-lasting, effective, and game-changing strategic partnership between their industry and its representative association.

Of course, industry growth is far easier to talk about than to achieve. Finding the right strategic partner is a first step toward your industry's unique opportunity. In the next five chapters we will look at industries that have found their champions in their own trade associations. We will see that trade associations can and do operate as strategic partners with the industries they represent; they can and do serve as the face of their industries; and they can and do help entire industries to achieve extraordinary growth even in the toughest times.

3 Recreational Boating and the Great Outdoors

Recreational boating is an extremely popular American pastime. The call of the outdoors has always had a strong pull on our national psyche. There's something of the frontier spirit in us that lures us out to hunt and fish and explore and enjoy our vast and beautiful patchwork of rivers, creeks, lakes, waterways, and bays, from sea to shining sea.

The industry fuels a powerful economic engine. According to the National Marine Manufacturers Association (NMMA), there are more than 35,000 marine businesses (including some 3,000 manufacturers, 11,200 marinas, and 15,000 dealers) that support approximately 700,000 jobs (including 111,000 in manufacturing and 78,500 at marinas), which generates about $170 billion in annual output (including $20.5 billion in tax revenue) in the United States.[1]

It is popular: In 2019 there were 11,878,542 registered recreational boating vessels in the United States,[2] and 141.6 million Americans go boating every year.[3]

It is inclusive: 62 percent of boat owners have an annual income of $100,000 or less, and 95 percent of boats in the United States are small, towable boats sized at 26 feet or less.[4]

And it is homegrown: 95 percent of boats sold in America are made in America.[5]

For more than 20 years, American recreational boating has been to a great extent influenced, guided, and strengthened by the NMMA, which has successfully positioned itself as *the industry*. "NMMA is the industry. We don't exist apart," said Thom Dammrich, who recently retired as president of NMMA. Recreational boating industry leaders, many of whom serve on the NMMA board, are fully committed to strategic partnerships. Thanks to their tireless leadership and unrelenting efforts over the past couple of decades, the NMMA today can itself be aptly described as a genuine strategic partnership among its members: a tightly knit group of friends and associates who are fierce competitors but who understand and are committed to the adage that a rising tide lifts all boats.[6]

The Inestimable Value of Relationships, Part 1

In 1999, the NMMA board of directors selected Dammrich to lead the association based on his perspective on strategic partnerships and his extraordinary ability to forge alliances. They respected his understanding of the vital role that relationships play in every aspect of human life and especially his effective navigation of relationships in business.

As a newcomer to the industry, Dammrich understood he needed to work hard to win acceptance. He recalls his earliest days as he tried to launch a new and different vision "I felt like I was an organ transplant the body was trying to reject." Kris Carroll, president of Grady-White, contacted Dammrich and served as a mentor who provided honest and sometimes tough feedback. Ms. Carroll would call him every week and say, "You've got a problem. You have a problem with this person or that person. You need to give this person a call."

Dammrich appreciated Ms. Carroll's mentorship and would immediately contact the person in question and establish a relationship. Every time Ms. Carroll called over the next two years, Dammrich sprang into action, building one relationship at a time. Dammrich views this as a breakthrough point early in his tenure at NMMA.

He took advantage of the opportunity to help executives get to know him, and they saw firsthand that he was sincere and wanted to understand their concerns. In every conversation, he also helped everyone understand why NMMA was doing what it was doing, and worked until he earned their trust and enlisted them in a new, different, and compelling vision for the industry.

As is the case for every new CEO, there are many ups and downs in the first two years. Dammrich recalls receiving a letter that said the association was "living in an ivory tower, and not connected to the industry." NMMA was located in the AON Building with a very favorable lease at the time. Dammrich called the executive, heard him out, and shared the background. Today, Dammrich fondly recalls that he and the industry executive worked through the situation and became good friends.

There was another major obstacle. At a meeting, staff complained that the trade press was writing constant negative stories about NMMA. Dammrich put together a list of 10 myths about NMMA

that the press was perpetuating and invited them all to meet with him
in Chicago. He addressed each of the 10 myths head on and demonstrated that he would have honest and open communication with
the trade press. Relationships began to form, trust began to build,
and the stories keeping the negative myths about NMMA alive
went away.

Again, he created an opportunity to bring everyone together and
start a dialogue. He had learned a lesson earlier in his career that he
would apply in building relationships with the trade press: "If you
leave a vacuum of information, they're going to fill it, and not always
with positive information about NMMA." From there forward,
Dammrich was extraordinarily accessible to the trade press. For the
next 20 years, he would talk to anybody, anytime, about anything.

Dammrich would continue to build upon his commitment like
this: "Part of my philosophy always was NMMA—*the industry*—
needs to be at every table where issues being discussed affect boating.
And so, we built relationships everywhere. Everywhere."

The Inestimable Value of Relationships, Part 2

Dammrich would have additional opportunities to unite the industry. When he attended his first NMMA annual conference, he had a
seminal moment. Yamaha Marine president at the time, Phil Dyskow,
approached him and said, "The fisheries associations in this country are all disjointed. They don't work together. There's no common
voice. You have to bring fishing organizations together." Dammrich
wondered how he would ever do this. But he began by getting
involved with fishing issues and fishing organizations.

He assumed the NMMA seat on the American Sportfishing Association (ASA) board and developed a close relationship with ASA CEO Mike Nussman. He got himself appointed to the Recreational Boating & Fishing Foundation (RBFF) board and the Sportfish and Boating Partnership Council (SBPC), where he regularly interacted with other leaders in the fishing industry, such as the head of All Waters Fishing Association (AFWA). He also engaged with the Recreational Fishing Alliance (RFA). And when the Coastal Conservation Association (CCA) suggested forming a coalition of saltwater fishing organizations, Dammrich made sure NMMA was first in line to support and finance the organization to unite fishing and boating interests.

He recalls sitting on 15 different boards of directors at one point in his career, including (among quite a few others) the International Council of Marine Industry Associations (ICOMIA), the American Boat & Yacht Council (ABYC), ASA, RBFF, and SBPC. Today, Dammrich is chairman of the board of directors of the Center for Sportfishing Policy (CSP), and he continues to serve on the RBFF board.

"We were everywhere," he told me. "Our board members and staff had personal input into just about every decision that was going to impact us." NMMA was represented on the ABYC technical board, on international standards committees, even on the recreational sector group in the European Union. "We were everywhere we needed to be!" he remembers exuberantly.

And it wasn't just sitting on boards of directors that captured NMMA's time and attention. The association's senior team raised the bar for strategic partnerships. They made themselves useful and available, and sometimes indispensable, to people up and down the entire supply chain. "We got ourselves ingrained with the dealers, with the distributors, with the marinas, with the boating safety people, with the boating access people," Dammrich recalls. "There wasn't a part of the industry where we were not involved, engaged, and welcome."

And it paid off. Especially when the chips were down. Their approach was intentionally selfless: "We always tried to give, and help everybody else, never asking for anything in return. And then along came Miami [a story we will elaborate later], and we needed help. And we weren't accustomed to asking for help, but we needed help. So, we reached out to all these people that we'd been helping over the years, and said, 'We need your help. Can you contact these members of Congress? Can you contact these state legislators? Can you get your members to do this . . . or that?' Not one person hesitated to say, 'Yes. We will do it.'"

Section One: Recreational Boating Is an Ecosystem

Sometime back in 2004, Dammrich had an epiphany. He was able to clearly articulate an idea that had been percolating ever since he'd had to deal almost unilaterally with a proposed lemon law in Connecticut. For some reason, most of the manufacturers were either unaware of the legislative assault on manufacturing or hadn't really thought about it. And when Dammrich approached the executive director of the MTA (marine trade association) in Connecticut for assistance, he was rebuffed. He was told it was a manufacturers issue (not the MTA's issue), so no—they were not going to help.

NMMA defeated the law, but the experience left Dammrich a bit cold, and miffed. The reaction by those not directly involved seemed rather short-sighted. Dammrich and his team began to ponder the problem.

Not long after that, during a Grow Boating meeting, Dammrich was struck with the realization that the industry is an ecosystem. It comprises many different parts: manufacturers (boats, engines, accessories), dealers, distributors, big box retailers, publications, yacht brokers, and others, like state MTAs. It made sense to those present. And so, they started to build a diagram (see Figure 3.1). Looking it over, Dammrich remarked, "If any part of this ecosystem is being attacked, or being hurt, it is eventually going to hurt the entire industry."

He reminded everyone of the argument he had made earlier in the year: "If that lemon law passes, that increases manufacturers' costs, which increases the cost of the product. We know that the demand for the product is highly elastic, so if the price goes up, dealers are going to sell fewer boats. And if the dealers sell fewer boats,

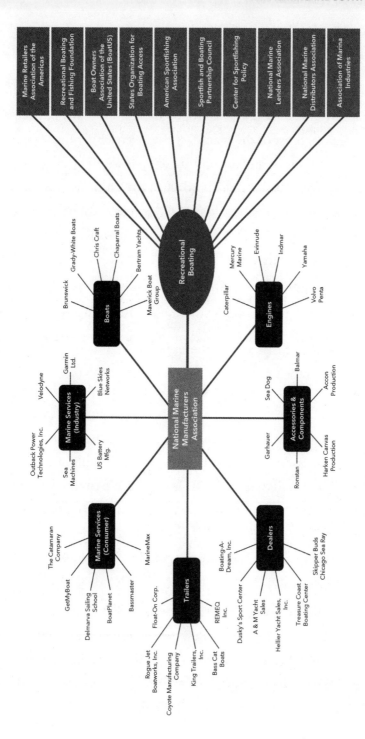

Figure 3.1 The Recreational Boating Industry Ecosystem

Source: Illustration artwork prepared by Erin Wagner, Edge Research.

that's fewer boat slips that are needed for those boats; that's fewer accessories that are needed for those boats. That means there are fewer accessories going through distribution." He systematically went down the whole list and then concluded, "Adversely affect one part of the industry, it will adversely affect everybody in the industry."

Dammrich later expounded further on the topic. "We've got environmental regulations on marinas, copper and stormwater runoff regulations that cost them a fortune. We [the manufacturers], fought those battles with them because if marina costs go up, the cost of boating goes up. So, people leave boating. Or people don't buy a boat. People don't buy a boat, that boat doesn't get manufactured; accessories don't get built for it. You can take any piece of the industry and come up with a negative scenario for that piece of the industry, and figure out that if that part of the industry is damaged, the whole industry gets damaged."

The team concluded that genuine strategic partnership must necessarily mean ownership for every aspect of the industry. Thus, "And everybody bought into that ecosystem concept to the point that it was no longer ours. It was everybody's. And that was perfect."

Delivering Value: The Customer Comes First

We are the industry is about the industry, the companies, and what they must achieve year over year. Regardless of the depth of the challenge, it means putting the industry first in all things, especially when it means lost revenue or jobs. In 2016, the Miami Convention Center was closed to undergo extensive renovations and remodeling. The Miami International Boat Show, one of NMMA's most prodigious enterprises, was celebrating its 75th anniversary that year. It requires one million square feet of show space. Now it had to be moved else-where, but still within Miami-Dade County, because you can hardly call it the Miami Boat Show if it is not at least pretty close to Miami. It turned out to be quite an undertaking. The change in venue was initially "met with some trepidation by exhibitors."[7]

The Miami Marine Stadium Park and Basin on Virginia Key turned out to be an outstanding alternative, but the transition was not without some hair-raising snags and difficulties, as we'll see later. For the moment, however, let us consider the venture from a high-level strategic perspective.

> "We are the industry. Every decision we make is on behalf of the industry."
>
> —Thom Dammrich

Recalling the experience of moving the Miami Boat Show, Dam-mrich made some rather poignant observations. "Frankly, just look-ing at it from the association point of view, not the industry point of view (although I truly believe they are one and the same in the case of NMMA), NMMA was worse off moving the show. NMMA would probably have been better off if we'd just thrown up our hands and said, 'We can't do this.'"

"But the industry would not have been better off, because the industry sells $500 million worth of product at that show. At least. There are a number of companies who without the Miami Boat Show would go out of business because they do 40 percent or 50 percent of their annual sales at that show. The industry needed that show. So, NMMA needed to do whatever we had to do to make sure we still had that show."

In short, the customer (or in this case, the association member—or, more precisely, the strategic partner) comes first. Even at the (considerable) expense of the association, the partnership comes first. And it worked out for the good of all, not only for the customer, but even more importantly for the customer's customer. The show was a success.

"Whether it was the gorgeous weather, exhibitors reporting significant sales, attendees having a blast enjoying the outdoor venue and all the new on-water features, or the more than 100,000 people from around the world who not only shopped our show but brought all-important tourism dollars to Miami-Dade—this year's show was the start of something very big for our industry and for South Florida,"[8] said Dammrich.

The Importance of Business Acumen, Part 1

Things were not all smooth and rosy behind the scenes of the change in venue for the Miami Boat Show. Dammrich describes some of the conference calls with the executive committee as "amazing" and "unbelievable" (not in a good way; these words were said with almost a shiver). "We were bleeding cash."

One particularly harrowing incident stands out in his memory. "I'll never forget a call in November [of 2015; the boat show was scheduled for February 11–15, 2016]. I was at METSTRADE, the leisure marine equipment industry show in Amsterdam, and I got a call from Cathy Rick-Joule [vice president of boat shows for the NMMA and longtime director of the Miami show]. And she said, 'Thom, we have to make a decision this week to spend a million dollars to buy all the electrical equipment we need to electrify the docks for the marina. And we don't have our permit yet. We don't know yet if we're going to get our permit. If we spend a million dollars and the show's canceled, we just wasted a million dollars. If we don't spend a million dollars and the show happens, we won't have any electricity on the docks. So, what are we going to do?'"

Within a couple of hours, NMMA managed to assemble the entire executive committee for an international teleconference to discuss the situation. This was no small feat on such short notice, because the CEOs were spread all over the globe at the time, including several in Amsterdam for the METSTRADE show. "I presented it to them. It took them 30 seconds to say, 'We've got to spend the money. We understand the situation. We've got to spend the money.' This is one of the things I love about working with trade associations, with guys who run their own companies: they get business. And they don't really have much patience for people who don't understand business in their association."

Business acumen really does matter for strategic partnerships to flourish. "The members will provide the money to do what they want done if what we're doing is delivering them value."

The Efficacy of Impartiality, Honest Communication, and Trust

When NMMA first started talking about who might take over the helm after he retired, Dammrich initially identified candidates he regarded as potential successors, professionals he thought could grow into the position. After about six months, however, the executive committee told him they were not as sanguine about the people he had identified. One of the primary reasons they cited was a strong desire to find someone who, like Dammrich, could be trusted to think strategically, communicate honestly, and remain impartial.

One board member observed, "Nobody ever knows what your position is because you spend all your time listening and pushing us and helping us all get to a collective point that we can all agree on. And the reason you're able to do that is because neither side views you as already being on the other side." The executive committee approved of those qualities in particular and deemed them essential for industry leadership—and for good reason.

Dammrich recalls facilitating a meeting between the manufacturers and the dealers "during a period of time when manufacturer and dealer relationships were still pretty tense. They didn't get along all that well." An issue with the Coast Guard had come up relating to the definition of the model year and how it would be assigned to recreational boats. There was a regulation on the books that the Coast Guard never enforced. In fact, they'd put out a circular on the subject that said they would not enforce it.

Then one day the head of the Coast Guard office of boating safety decided for some still-obscure reason that he wanted to enforce the regulation, and "the manufacturers revolted. They wanted to come up with a new definition of model year." Of course, what the manufacturers wanted was not exactly what the dealers wanted, and a kerfuffle ensued. The Coast Guard boating safety director promised Dammrich that if he could somehow get the dealers and the manufacturers—and BoatUS (which represents the consumers)—to all agree on a single position, he would do it.

Dammrich arranged for a full-day meeting in Chicago with the manufacturers and dealers. And the meeting did in fact take the full day.

"Everybody presented their point of view," he recalls, "over and over and over again." He just kept asking questions, prompting discussion, and listening carefully to try to figure out how he could possibly move this group to agreement across what seemed to be such a vast chasm: to figure out the endpoint that would be acceptable (and hopefully agreeable) to both sides.

He attributes the success of that meeting to his unswerving commitment to the industry as a whole. "We were only able to [reach an agreement] because in spite of the fact that we were working with the manufacturers, the dealers did not see me as advocating for the manufacturers in that meeting. We were advocating for the industry: looking for the best solution for everybody." And everyone knew it. And everybody trusted both his thinking and his motives.

"There were times in the meeting," Dammrich says, "when I would advocate the dealer point of view, and times I would advocate the manufacturer point of view, without ever letting on as to what my own personal opinion was." It was an effective approach. It built trust.

Dammrich mentions one point during the meeting when Joe Hoffmaster (past chairman of the Marine Retailers Association) got up to stretch his legs. "He walked over to me and said, 'Thom, keep going. You're getting there.' And we got there. We got an agreement." That meeting marked a turning point in how the association understood itself. The members truly began to see themselves as a strategic partnership.

Dammrich took the agreement that the manufacturers and dealers had forged to BoatUS, and got them to sign off on it, too. He then took it (triumphantly) back to the Coast Guard. The Coast Guard boating safety official apparently never believed for a moment that such an agreement could be struck because after it was accomplished, he reneged on his promise. True to form, the NMMA's power team of industry leaders did not take the betrayal sitting down. "We went to Congress and got the U.S. Coast Guard reauthorization to include our definition of the model year. In the end, the government served the people."

Two Are Better Than One: The Ineluctable Power of Partnership

There's another aspect of the nature of associations as strategic partnerships that Dammrich extols as a splendid side benefit and a delight to watch. CEOs of small, entrepreneurial, family-owned marine businesses sit together in the executive committee with CEOs of billion-dollar companies as friends and equals, not as competitors (even though they may in fact be intense competitors). They like each other. Everyone operates on an equal basis and embraces the notion that decisions made by the board of directors have opportunity or consequence for the entire industry. And participation in it is tremendously valuable to all of them.

It is a dynamic that is not easily duplicated, and one that cannot be faked. And they learn from each other. Executives willingly share examples of how their service on the board helped them learn and evolve as executives. It requires conscious, intentional effort. When it happens, the impact of the synergy created can be astonishing.

Commitment Matters

Another fundamental principle that the NMMA team took seriously in their quest to design and mold the recreational boating (and fishing) industry into one vast strategic partnership is the principle of high-level engagement at the highest levels of participation.

Dammrich regarded it as indispensable that association board members have authority to commit their respective companies to decisions and actions. Normally, though not always, that's CEO level.

When Dammrich first joined NMMA, there were a lot of vice presidents on the NMMA board and on the three division boards (the Boat Manufacturer Division, the Engine Manufacturer Division, and the Marine Accessory and Component Division). One of the first decisions he made was to recruit CEOs onto all the division boards, because those boards feed the NMMA board, and to put CEOs in the chairs of all these divisions, because they become the chairs of the NMMA board.

The NMMA leadership team never explicitly required CEO participation, but they did expect board members to speak with full authority without checking with someone not sitting at the table. In other words, if the NMMA board is voting to do a special assessment of every member (equal, for example, to 50 percent of their annual dues), board members need to be able to participate in the conversation knowing with certainty that they can commit their company to invest in industry initiatives. In most cases that's the CEO. So, that level of participation is what they worked toward, and that is for the most part what they got.

Operating at the 50,000-foot level, board members embrace NMMA as the industry because decisions they make help to influence and shape the business environment they operate in at the state, local, national, and international levels.

Looking back, industry leaders are satisfied that it was the right approach and that it worked admirably. "We went from complete disinterest in the NMMA board and governance to the point where we could not accommodate every CEO that wanted to be engaged."

The Impact of the 2020 Pandemic

The NMMA leadership team's extraordinary insight, foresight, and preparation have positioned the recreational boating industry excellently for just such a time as this. Indeed, the industry is currently booming in the midst of a pandemic, largely due to their efforts because they understand the real power of strategic partnerships and the relationships necessary to make them work.

NMMA reported in mid-September 2020 that "47 percent of marine manufacturers saw a year-over-year increase in new orders, and 15 percent reported substantial growth in sales."[9]

Buzz Watkins, the owner of Lakeway's MarineMax Sail & Ski, said that "People figured out that boating is one of the things they can do with their family and properly enjoy the outdoors and be socially distant."[10]

My friend Dave Reich, owner of Coastal Marine in Reedville, Virginia, told me that the summer of 2020 was one of the busiest summers he can remember in his 32 years of selling and repairing boats in the Northern Neck. And he is always busy. "It's been a crazy year trying to keep up with demand. With the pandemic going on, people were coming in droves for me to fix their boats and to buy used boats so they could get away from the city and enjoy the Chesapeake Bay. I've been running around like a jack rabbit, but it's worth it to see my customers so happy during such trying times."

Industry analysts in the boating community have commented on a few rather interesting facts about boat buying in the first year of the pandemic:

- First-time boat buyers entered the market in record numbers.

- 20 percent more boats were sold in June 2020 than in June 2019.

- More boat orders for future delivery were placed in 2020 than in 2019.[11]

- Unit sales in 2020 exceeded 300,000 units, a number last reached in 2007 (prior to the global financial crisis), and a number most in the industry felt would never be reached again.

The onslaught of COVID-19 had the boating industry in some disarray in the spring of 2020. "By mid-April, sales slumped, and production slowed. Some manufacturers furloughed employees, or temporarily shuttered, to better clarify the uncertainty that was to come for their production lines. [And] the outlook for the summer appeared to worsen. But something happened few anticipated. Society pivoted outdoors."[12] By summertime, it had come roaring back.

We'll look at one of the reasons why that happened in just a moment. But first let's have a look at another ecosystem.

Section Two: Outdoor Recreation Is an Even Bigger Ecosystem

The Outdoor Recreation Roundtable (ORR) bills itself as "America's leading coalition of outdoor recreation trade associations and organizations working to promote the growth of the outdoor recreation economy and outdoor recreation activities." In fact, it is a great web of interlocking strategic partnerships.

ORR was originally the brainchild of a group of boating and fishing association executives (including Thom Dammrich) who were seeking to extend their ecosystem to include all outdoor recreation. They believed (and now know) that what is good for outdoor recreation is good for boating and fishing, and vice versa.

The roundtable played a critical role in elevating the industry's relevance to the economy. Today the U.S. Department of Commerce's Bureau of Economic Analysis (BEA) recognizes it. The annual reports reflect the contributions of outdoor recreation and the recreational boating industry to the U.S. economy. The industry ecosystem demonstrated the impact of coming together through strategic partnerships to position the industry for long-term growth (see Figure 3.2). Dammrich credits ORR as the linchpin that helped achieve the BEA's recognition of outdoor recreation as a vital contributor to U.S. gross domestic product (GDP).

"ORR members represent the thousands of businesses that produce vehicles, equipment, gear, apparel and services for the 144 million Americans who enjoy our national parks, waterways, byways, trails, and outdoor spaces."[13]

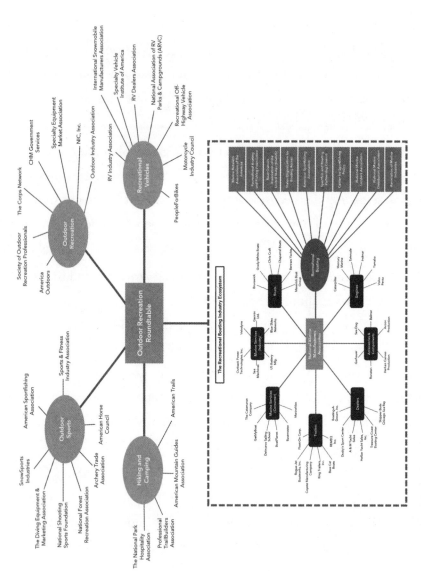

Figure 3.2 The Outdoor Recreation Industry Ecosystem
Source: Illustration artwork prepared by Erin Wagner, Edge Research.

The outdoor recreation industry is an "overlooked economic giant."[14] It makes up 2.1 percent of U.S. GDP.[15] It is said that "outdoor recreation exceeds such industries as mining and agriculture, which combined, have a lower contribution [to the U.S. economy] than outdoor recreation."[16]

America Races to the Outdoors

It was not only the recreational boating industry that was initially adversely affected by the advent of the pandemic. Small businesses across the nation were struggling mightily to stay afloat.

The strategic partnership relationships that had been developed over the years within the ORR were galvanized, and the spirit of cooperation among a network of CEOs across the vast outdoor recreation industry kicked into high gear.

Some weeks into the initial turbulence of the COVID-19 outbreak in the United States in early 2020, Dammrich (despite his September 2019 retirement from NMMA) began to do a few of the things that he does best: make connections, bring people together, and rally the troops.

He had received a call from a retired Brunswick Corporation executive (manufacturers of such world-renowned marine brands as Mercury engines, Boston Whaler, SeaRay, Harris, and Bayliner), who had been talking with the chairman of Thor Industries (the world's largest RV manufacturer). Together they had hatched an idea, in response to the pandemic tumult, that it would be great if the RV industry and the boating industry could put their resources together and do some sort of joint campaign to get our nation out of doors: something along the lines of, "You've been cooped up for 10 weeks.

Now is the time to get out and enjoy some recreation. Go boating, go RVing, take advantage of the great outdoors!"

Dammrich called Frank Peterson, CEO and president at RBFF (famous for the Take Me Fishing consumer outreach campaign) and encouraged him to take a leadership role and work with Discover Boating to build a really strong coalition, with everybody coming together to get people outdoors. Frank thought it a great idea and began to contact other industry leaders to widen the spectrum of participation and garner more support.

Dammrich also reached out to the new NMMA president, Frank Hugelmeyer, who had previously directed the GoRVing promotion strategy at the RV Industry Association (RVIA), which was a smashing success and had increased RV sales dramatically in years prior.

The ball got rolling.

The Importance of Business Acumen, Part 2

The two Franks agreed to work on a joint Discover Boating/Take Me Fishing effort. They decided not to focus the campaign on future buyers because in the current crisis the boating industry folk needed sales immediately. It became clear that the focus ought to be on getting people who already own boats out on the water, using their boats (so they'll be buying more accessories), and on the baby boomers, who are still buying most of the boats. "You've got to get to the current audience of people who are buying," Thom Dammrich remembers counseling them, "not people who are going to buy in two or three years. Two or three years isn't going help anybody today. And they need help today."

"You've got to be constantly balancing what the industry needs long term," says Dammrich, "and where we need to move the industry long term. But we also need to clearly understand what the industry needs today—right now—because if we don't give them what they need today, there isn't going to be a long term." That is the kind of thinking that guided the industry through the great recession; it is what guided NMMA through the great Miami challenge; and it is what is guiding outdoor recreation industry leaders through the current situation.

The combined resources and creativity of that immense and popular and powerful industry coalition turned the COVID-19 pandemic—an incredibly dangerous and destructive force in the economy and in society at large—into a boon for outdoor recreation businesses, while at the same time providing a healthy alternative for people who were desperately struggling to maintain some semblance of normalcy in exceedingly dire and unpredictable times.

The recreational boating industry was a beacon of opportunity for consumers in 2020. Frank Hugelmeyer, NMMA president, celebrated the industry's success despite the global pandemic: "For the first time in more than a decade, we saw an increase in first-time boat buyers, who helped spur growth of versatile, smaller boats—less than 26 feet—that are often towed to local waterways and provide a variety of boating experiences, from fishing to watersports."

To survive and prosper in troubled times depends on maintaining the ability to serve your industry both now and later. It requires a deep understanding of what exactly is happening and how precisely it is impacting every part of the industry ecosystem today. And it may require making sacrifices in order provide unexpected and sometimes counterintuitive investment in the industry to keep it alive and well on its trajectory into the future.

The Importance of Industry Data, Part 1

Helping the recreational boating industry remain durable has a lot to do with data and how it helps manufacturers and the supply chain manage their businesses. One of the many skills Dammrich brought with him when he took over NMMA all those years ago was a thorough understanding of macroeconomic data and its influence on business decisions. Dammrich connected the dots. He wanted to help the industry understand the key macroeconomic factors that are influencers of boat sales.

Dammrich asked his statistics team to look at key economic indicators, including housing starts, to determine how they track against boat sales. They sought correlations among each of the following economic indicators: automobile sales, recreational vehicle sales, unemployment, GDP growth, and consumer confidence. Interestingly enough, they found a direct correlation between each of these factors and boat sales. At his direction, NMMA regularly reported this data to the industry.

The data reports served as an important resource to educate the industry because they helped guide business decisions. Dammrich said, "If the outlook that economists are predicting is GDP growth, low unemployment, and increasing consumer confidence, we can probably predict [that] things are going to be good for another two years. On the other side, when consumer confidence would turn down, U.S. GDP would start to slow down, and unemployment would start to rise, we would tell them to watch these things because this is telling you to put the brakes on a little bit."

In his first four to five months as NMMA president, Dammrich recalls a meeting with a member of his statistics team where he was informed that "inventory is building up relative to sales, sales are slowing down and inventory is building up, I think the industry is going to have a problem."

Steeped deeply in transparency, Dammrich wanted to share this information with the industry and released it all via press release. However, he made sure the release reported that it was only an observation, and encouraged the industry to keep an eye on what NMMA was seeing. In his communications, he emphasized that the industry should keep an eye on this information. He emphasized, "I didn't say stop production or what to do about it; I just said here are some facts, and you ought to pay attention to them."

A couple of months later, Dammrich had a meeting with George Buckley, chairman and CEO of Brunswick Corporation at the time. Dammrich remembers this first meeting, during which Mr. Buckley said, "That press release you put out was irresponsible. You better be right because I cut production." Dammrich was gratified when events confirmed his expectations and justified Mr. Buckley's decision to cut production.

As a data-driven executive, Dammrich used data throughout his NMMA tenure to help the industry make informed business decisions. He felt it important to present information that enabled good business decisions. "We gave people the facts for better or for worse. And when we thought all of the indicators were headed in the right direction, we told people things are going to be good for a couple of years." At the same time, "When we saw things going in the wrong direction we told people, 'keep an eye on this, there is trouble ahead.'"

The Importance of Industry Data, Part 2

NMMA also used data to promote the industry directly to its consumers through the media. During the boat show season, Dammrich and his team delivered pertinent facts on the value of the industry in four to five interviews each week. He had to know the industry and its statistics, and he needed to understand the data inside and out to effectively communicate high impact story lines in these interviews.

Since NMMA is the industry, Dammrich regularly communicated to the American public. He emphasized how important the boating industry is to outdoor recreation, and how it is a driver of overall economic health. And he conveyed time and time again how important the industry is to local communities.

Through this effort, NMMA used new and compelling data every year. It was so effective that the same reporters, year after year, would stay connected with the association to keep current on new and emerging industry trends. ORR data was also incorporated into the larger narrative that industry and NMMA utilized to inform and engage consumers.

Shaping the External Environment

Earlier we learned about the ORR achieving recognition by the BEA. Having the ability to share this data in conversations with regulators and legislators is significant. Every conversation with elected officials and regulators is fact-based, informative, and relevant.

Dammrich buoyantly notes that "having this data and using it in industry association coalitions, and later with the Outdoor Recreation Roundtable, was huge. It changed the game for the industry."

Based on Dammrich's assessment, the industry would always do the right things, and unnecessary costs were avoided. Advocacy was the vehicle to prevent the industry from being burdened with unnecessary costs. He worked to make sure that "government at all levels took actions that would support the success of these businesses as central to NMMA's role." There were always regulatory efforts that tended to impede the industry's progress, but over time, the foundation of relationships and data built an advocacy juggernaut. It was capable of pushing back against efforts to ban watercraft or restrict access to fisheries and waterways.

All these efforts were important to the overall health of the industry. On occasion, the association would interface with as many as 15 different federal agencies. The list of agencies included the Department of Commerce on Trade and Tariffs and Fisheries, the Department of Agriculture and Forest Service to maintain or expand access to fisheries, the Army Corps of Engineers because they manage the lion's share of water and lakes issues in the United States, Department of the Interior, the Bureau of Land Management, the EPA, OSHA, and so forth.

From a "raging fire down to a smoldering ash, we were always in the trenches. Unfortunately, the government's first solution to every problem is to ban it. It's not the best management method and that's why the industry increased its financial investment over time to make sure NMMA had the resources it needed to effectively make its case."

Some of the challenges included crafts ranging from ski boats to wakeboard boats where newly installed ballast tanks would create more weight. Homeowners in and around lakes expressed concerns that the additional tanks created too much weight, created erosion, and were destroying the shorelines. NMMA addressed these concerns—and others like them—both on their own and through coalition efforts.

Summing Up

From Dammrich's vantage point, NMMA had two key roles. One was to influence the macroenvironment to help the industry be successful. And the other was to help his members sell more boats. He applied both strategies to help the recreational boating industry survive the great recession. And even though Dammrich had retired, the pieces were in place to help the industry thrive through a global pandemic.

The recreational boating industry, working through and with its strategic partner NMMA, has become more durable and has increased its economic footprint. This is an industry that now engages almost one-third of the population in the United States in recreational boating.

According to the United States Coast Guard, 61 percent of boaters have an annual income of $75,000 or less.[18] Recreational boating's appeal is broader, and the industry hopes to increase its reach from now on. And the U.S. Bureau of Economic Analysis reports that boating and fishing are now the largest conventional activities in the United States, totaling $23.6 billion in current value added.[19]

NMMA leaders spend a lot of time listening to their members, gauging how circumstances are affecting them, and trying to understand what the industry needs to be successful. And then—even in the most difficult times—they make sure that the association invests money on the things they need to spend money on to help the industry continue to be successful, not only in the moment, but in the long run. They are always looking to the future and never hesitate to do what seems prudent to prepare the industry for whatever might come.

Strategic partnership is a lifelong journey for Thom Dammrich. When he recently took the helm as chairman of the Center for Sportfishing Policy (CSP), an organization he helped found 15 years ago in order to "unite the recreational fishing and boating industries," the official announcement mentioned some of Dammrich's latest achievements: "In 2018, Thom Dammrich was inducted into the NMMA Hall of Fame, and in 2019, he received CSP's Eddie Smith Manufacturer of the Year Award for his dedication to the recreational boating industry and his commitment to angler access and marine conservation. In 2019, he was also inducted into the ASA Hall of Fame, and the Boating Safety Hall of Fame."[20]

Dammrich, together with the industry leaders he served with on various boards of directors, his own NMMA board, and his exceptionally talented senior team, quite literally and quite intentionally transformed the recreational boating industry particularly and the larger outdoor recreation industry generally. They did it by building and leveraging strong, vibrant, and lasting strategic partnerships within and among industry and trade associations. It is a remarkable legacy of which they are rightfully proud.

4 Baking

Bread has been a part of our shared experience from time immemorial. Buns and biscuits and cakes and pies, too, have nourished, sustained, and delighted people for many centuries. And while bakers have always gathered to share tips, techniques, and formulas, it was the professional bakers in early medieval Europe who were among the first tradesmen to create formal guilds to protect trade secrets and help one another succeed. Enduring relationships are the firm foundation on which baked goods and the baking industry have been built from the beginning.

A key part of that foundation is the industry's relationship with its consumers and their ever-evolving tastes. As in any consumer-facing industry, "customers have the biggest impact on strategy."[1] And since they do, companies and executives pore over data to understand how to position the products they will bring to the marketplace.

The Baking Industry Supply Chain

Because bakers have always intuitively understood not only the importance of lasting relationships but also the incredible multiplying effect of a little bit of yeast properly mixed into dough, today they lead a powerful, durable, and far-reaching coalition of companies with (sometimes surprising and unexpected) shared interests.

The baking industry supply chain includes farmers, growers, and producers of grains, flour, sugar, and spices; artificial and natural flavors and ingredients; fruits and nuts and butter and milk and eggs and salt. And that is only the food side of the equation. Then there are the manufacturers of machinery (from dough mixers, sheeters, dividers, and presses to bun and sheet pan racks and dollies; from bread slicers and graters to convection ovens, deck ovens, and digital water meters).

Additionally, it includes the chemical manufacturers (from food grade lubricants to pest control products) and the packaging manufacturers. ("Baked goods deteriorate due to staling, water loss or gain, oxidation, and microbial growth . . . . Packaging to extend shelf life to preserve consumer spending dollars, decrease food waste, and increase food safety is being addressed using three main packaging technologies: barriers, modified atmosphere packaging (MAP), and freezer-compatible packaging."[2]) And, of course, there are transportation and logistics, facilities engineering, food safety research, education and training, government regulation, and much more. But that should suffice to give an overall sense of the baking industry writ large.

According to "The Baking Industry 2020 Economic Impact Study," the industry provided jobs directly for almost 765,000 highly skilled people and directly contributed more than $154 billion to the economy in 2020. Indirectly, the industry was responsible for nearly 790,000 supplier jobs, which generated upward of $193 billion in economic activity. The industry's "induced impact" (that is, multiplier effect), which includes "daily spending by employees of the baking industry, and those of supplier firms whose jobs are directly dependent on baked product sales and production . . . on everything from housing, to food, to educational services and medical care,"[3] was estimated at more than $133 billion and generated approximately 742,000 jobs. The study concluded that all told, the baking industry contributes about $480.5 billion in economic output. That's about 2.46 percent of U.S. gross domestic product (GDP).

Regardless of economic conditions, people must eat. Baking products are consumer staples and are used every day. They also have a 98 percent household penetration. It's an industry that listens carefully and responds quickly to consumer preferences, and it's an industry that values and knows how to leverage all its relationships. What matters most to this vital sector is achieving its business outcomes by working collaboratively to shape the external business environment.

The American Bakers Association (ABA) has represented American commercial baking interests since 1897. It has worked tirelessly for decades "to increase protection from costly government overreach, build the talent pool of skilled workers with specialized training programs, and forge industry alignment by establishing a more receptive environment to grow the baking industry."[4] The baking industry is specifically defined here as "those firms involved in the production, distribution/importation, and retailing of baked goods including breads, cakes, pies, pastries, cookies, crackers, tortillas, pasta, pretzels, cereal and granola bars, baking mixes, and other bakery products."[5] It also includes pre-prepared dough and frozen bakery products manufacturers.[6]

Over the years, however, recognizing and responding to the fact that the bakers' fortunes are inextricably linked to the stability of the entire supply chain, the association expanded its membership to include suppliers to the baking industry and also to international bakeries and suppliers. Today, the ABA seeks to shape the business environment on behalf of a vast and complex network of interconnected and interdependent businesses stretching across a wide array of specializations, including bakers, suppliers (which they classify as allied), and international firms. See Figure 4.1.

ABA board leadership is mindful of the fact that every link in the supply chain must be protected and strengthened in order to ensure the bakers' success. Given the diversity of interests and needs represented up and down the supply chain, it's immediately apparent that just keeping lines of communication open is an impressive feat; recognizing and prioritizing outcomes that will benefit all parties, and then patiently and persistently building and maintaining broad support for those tasks is positively Herculean. It requires durable relationships.

Business Matters: Data and Analytics

When the board of directors sought to replace ABA's CEO in 1995, they sought a different approach, one that combined strategic relationships, business acumen, and something that elevated the industry well beyond advocacy. Their new leader had to be able to engage and interact with the entire industry, build a lasting platform that would transform the industry, and be able to build strategic alliances that could help to shape the business environment well into the future. With their selection of Robb MacKie, they identified a chief executive who, over time, could help the industry grow and compete. Today, in large part due to MacKie and a high-performing team, the board and the industry unmistakably see ABA as the centerpiece of their go-to-market strategies.

As a consumer-facing industry, they rely heavily on data and analytics to surface new and emerging trends in consumer attitudes and purchasing patterns. Throughout his 15-year tenure, MacKie and the

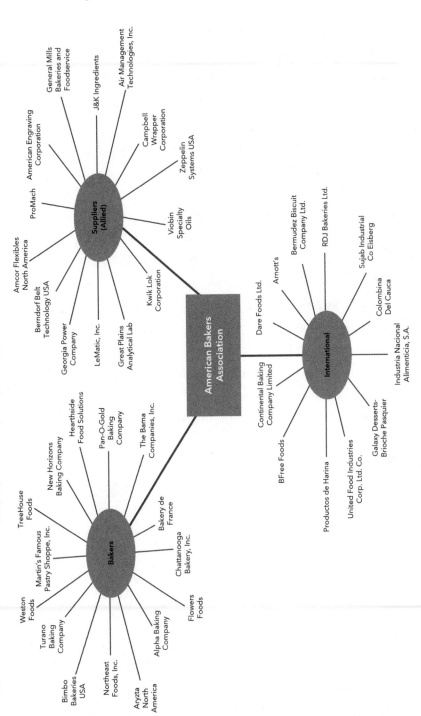

Figure 4.1 The Baking Industry Ecosystem

A small representation of the 300-plus members of the ABA—90 percent of which are small to medium-sized bakeries—who together make 85 percent of baked goods in the United States.[7]

Source: Illustration artwork prepared by Erin Wagner, Edge Research.

ABA team regularly rely on data to guide how they invest industry resources. They understand that any actions they take will invariably reach the consumer. MacKie related to me a little vignette that goes to the importance of data and analytics from a business perspective:

> I won't say that I reference the data every day, every week, maybe not even every month. But I know it's there; it's in the back of my mind. And I just used it today. We had our weekly senior management call, and we were doing a recap of the week. And I said to them, "Here's the big difference. When we did the industry survey, one of the big disconnects was when we asked the question, 'What does ABA mean for the industry?' We learned that 87 percent believe we are aligned with the industry. But when we asked, 'What does it mean for my company?' It was 70 percent. It was not bad." And I said, "If we were to ask those two questions today, I would guess we have closed that gap." And that's something that you can't overlook. Now we have that piece of the alignment. We already had broad alignment between ABA and the industry, and now we have ABA and the company.

This is why it is being done: Robb MacKie is aware of that simple data point. It floats in and out of his consciousness, but it never leaves him. And it causes him to act accordingly.

The Grain Chain

The Grain Chain, "a farm to table coalition of stakeholders in the grain industry sector,"[8] is another example of using strategic alliances to leverage supply chains. Chaired by the ABA, the Grain Chain has used strategic communication to considerable positive effect. Some of the coalition's important achievements include effectively communicating the message to Congress and across the federal government that "all grains, enriched refined and whole, are valuable contributors to our health."[9]

The Grain Chain was able to celebrate, for example, contributions to the *2020–2025 Dietary Guidelines for Americans* (DGAs), which is published by the USDA and HHS.

Christine Cochran, executive director of the Grain Foods Foundation, said of the effort, "The unity of the Grain Chain's message and the importance of its being heard have been affirmed in this DGA cycle today: the nutritional contribution of grains is essential in the diet at all stages of life."[10] Jane DeMarchi, president of the National Agri-Marketing Association, also lauded the inclusion of Grain Chain recommendations in the DGA: "We are delighted that the nutritional value of both whole and enriched grains in the diet, which is supported by vast scientific research, is acknowledged by the updated Dietary Guidelines. Grain foods are staples that create the foundation for a healthy and balanced diet."[11]

Strategic Relationships Matter (Again, Still, and Always)

The importance of relationships in forging successful strategic partnerships cannot be overestimated. You may recall that we identified alignment on values and outcomes as a core characteristic that predicts partnership success. While the ABA and the baking industry at large are in veritable lockstep, evolving consumer tastes and disruptive innovation requires a constant focus on maintaining that alignment. And it is being done.

ABA president and CEO MacKie attributes this alignment largely to some good decisions the association (at the behest and on behalf of the industry) made several years ago, which he acknowledges were partly purposeful and partly fortuitous; partly the result of hard work and partly just some good old-fashioned luck, but mostly purposeful hard work and preparation. The eminent immunologist Louis Pasteur once rightly said that chance favors the prepared mind.[12]

What certainly was a matter of preparation is the strategic plan developed by and for the baking industry back in 2017. The endeavor was undertaken with the conscious intention of strengthening communications and relationships with a view to developing bona fide strategic partnerships between ABA and its members and the industry, as well as with others across the supply chain.

For the purpose of our discussion, the three most significant ingredients of the baking industry strategic plan are these:

1. Pursue state government relations (to expand the industry's ability to shape the marketplace) with the same vim and vigor that have been applied to developing federal relationships for many years.

2. Initiate a strategic communications plan to promote the value of lifelong baking industry careers and attract skilled workers.

3. Align policy communications among supply chain organizations to reduce policy cost exposure and optimize support for the industry.

Shaping the Business Environment at the State Level

Recognizing the need to protect the industry's flank, ABA has taken an increasingly disciplined approach to expanding their reach and effectiveness at the state government level. Foregoing the mile-wide and inch-deep approach that can be tempting in such cases, MacKie chose instead to "take that focus and priority-setting that's been effective for us on the federal level to the state level. Only make it even more so." The mission, he decided, was "a couple of states, a couple of priority issues." This strategy has paid off handsomely for the industry.

Shaping the External Environment, Part 1

When Rich Scalise, the founder and CEO of Hearthside Food Solutions, decided that it was time to step down from running his company's day-to-day operations, he called his friend MacKie at ABA to let him know. He also told MacKie that they were hiring a long-time food industry professional named Chuck Metzger to replace himself. He wanted to make sure that Mr. Metzger—who was "a great guy," but "new to the whole association thing"—would get invested. Robb had an introductory phone call with Mr. Metzger, but before they could meet in person, the 2020 pandemic struck.

Shortly afterward, MacKie got a late-evening phone call from Mr. Metzger, who told him that if Hearthside didn't get relief from the work from home order in Michigan, they would not be able to open for business the next day. ABA went to work. They sent Mr. Metzger the industry documents certifying bakers as essential workers under federal guidelines (an early win for ABA at the federal level) and then reached out to the governor's office in Michigan. They were able to resolve the situation, and Hearthside was able to open the plant.

Two days later, Mr. Metzger encountered the exact same situation in Ohio. This time MacKie was confident they could sort it out quickly as they had developed excellent relationships with Governor

DeWine's office. "And sure enough, we worked our magic again," MacKie reported.

Mr. Metzger was impressed. He later confessed that he had been skeptical of associations ("I thought these were boondoggles to nice places"), but that Hearthside would not be in business today if not for ABA. He agreed to take Rich Scalise's seat on the ABA board. He'd gotten invested. Reflecting briefly after relating the story, MacKie told me, "We talk these big issues, big politics; when it's just solving those business challenges. And being able to deliver. It's invigorating."

As a side note, Erin Sharp of The Kroger Co. said this to MacKie: "Robb, you guys are delivering business solutions at the critical time. And aggressively pushing the critical infrastructure designation is probably what kept our business moving, operating. Absent that, we would probably be shut down."

Shaping the External Environment, Part 2

With a strong desire to help the industry, MacKie and his team sought to deliver quick wins in states around the United States. The first is the use of reusable plastic trays that are critical components of baking goods distribution. They are a safe, reliable, and durable method to bring finished products from plants to depots and commercial customers, and then they are returned to the plants. Organized tray theft is expensive, costing industry companies $10 million per year to replace the trays. Theft also results in operational and distribution disruption for baking companies. MacKie and his team saw this is an urgent call to action:

- Leading a powerful effort in the state of Maryland in 2013, ABA and its industry strategic partners organizations and members achieved successful passage of a new law that allows owners of reusable trays to bring civil action and recover damages resulting from theft. The new law also increased specified penalties and fines for offenders.

- Later, in 2019, through its state and local partnerships and its members including Bimbo Bakeries USA, Flowers Industries, Kroger, smaller companies, and state and local partnerships, the association went to the Texas state capitol in Austin to have new laws enacted that would prevent tray loss that cost the industry $5 million in losses on an annual basis. The legislation, spearheaded by the Texas Retailers Association with strong support from ABA, became law and applies criminal penalties to tray theft and allows civil recovery by prosecutors.

The second quick win has to do with New Jersey attempting to severely limit the operation of independent distributors in the state. Since half the industry utilizes independent distributors to get their products to the marketplace, ABA stepped in to support baking companies that include Amoroso's, Pepperidge Farm, Martin's Famous Potato Rolls and Bread, and several other companies. Through its focused efforts, the association thwarted this effort through alliances with nontraditional partners such as the newspaper and copywriter industry.

For the time being, legislative and regulatory activity is slower among the states, adds MacKie. Recognizing the change in presidential administrations, he sees activism as shifting to Washington, DC.

Noting the importance of an early warning system and prior conversations with Erin Sharp of The Kroger Co, MacKie agrees with her earlier guidance: "We're not going to win them all, but we now have a better idea of what's going on that we didn't know three or four years ago."

Alignment on Values and Outcomes

A large part of the ABA's successful strategic partnerships with an ever-expanding number of its members is rooted in shared vision, shared values, and a shared definition of desirable outcomes. These shared outcomes focus on shifting consumer attitudes, implementation of new technologies that maximize the efficiency of the supply chain, and deployment of workforce strategies to support the industry today and into the future.

Fred Penny is the president of Bimbo Bakeries USA, a subsidiary of Grupo Bimbo (the largest bakery company in the world, which recently celebrated its 75th anniversary). Mr. Penny is also a former board chairman of ABA. He attributes Grupo Bimbo's market dominance to the fact that "they have adhered closely to the mission of the founders, which is 'to build a highly productive and deeply humane company.' That's been the ethos that's guided the company."[13] Bimbo Bakeries USA describes its own beliefs as follows:[14]

- We value the person
- We are one community
- We get results
- We compete and win
- We are sharp operators
- We act with integrity
- We transcend and endure

Those are values that the ABA can get behind. And it has done so in both good times and troubled times. Fred Penny noted that the ABA executive committee had an emergency meeting at the beginning of the 2020 pandemic, and the entire industry rallied together and committed to a shared mission to protect all of the employees and do whatever it takes to keep America fed.

Mr. Penny extolled the baking industry, as well as others in the food space, for stepping up to the plate and publicly recognizing, honoring, and protecting their frontline associates while continuing to provide fresh food every day to feed our nation despite significant supply chain challenges.

Bill Paterakis, president and CEO, H&S Bakery, Schmidt Baking, Northeast Foods, and ABA board member, notes how important empathy is in a time of crisis: "It's important that you show your employees that you understand what they're going through. They're putting aside their personal fears and anxieties and coming to work."

Brad Alexander, COO at Flowers Foods and current ABA chairman of the board, shared a similar vision regarding his own company's approach: "During the crisis we really committed to three main priorities. The first was maintaining a safe workplace for and supporting our employees in every way possible. Two was fulfilling our obligation as a key part of the nation's food supply. And three is really supporting the communities that we serve."[15]

Mr. Alexander takes these priorities seriously. He notes that with regard to the first priority, "communication is the key—listening mostly. We're doing a lot of overcommunicating right now, letting employees know that they've been heard and that they're appreciated for their hard work."[16] He is also extremely proud of the job that Flowers' bakeries have been doing across the country. "They've always had a close connection with the communities they are located in," he said, "but they've continued to reach out and support those in need in these difficult times. Countless donations of food and supplies from our bakeries to local food banks, hospitals and first responders have been made around the country."[17]

Flowers Foods has indeed always charged all their bakeries to get involved in their local communities. And as Mr. Alexander puts it, "whether you're one [bakery], or 46 (like us), if you get involved in your community you can always help those in need. And that's part of our responsibility as corporate America."[18]

Flowers Foods shares many of the same values and takes the same general approach to relationships as ABA, Bimbo, and many more of ABA's member organizations. These shared values and shared goals have over time allowed ABA's leadership to forge strong and resilient personal relationships, which serve as the foundation for excellent strategic partnerships.

Attracting Skilled Workers

The baking industry's shared commitment to entice world-class talent into lifelong baking industry careers is another initiative that represents shared values and outcomes. And this, too, is bearing much fruit.

Alexander was recently discussing the trend toward continued automation in the baking industry "to make sure that we're as efficient as possible in our bakeries; to make sure that we give the best quality that we can to the consumer."[19] But even as he recognized the importance of automation, he was quick to point out that the workforce and employees will always matter more.

"[A] bakery is not a cookie cutter thing. Each day it's a little different. You'll have different temperatures in the bakery; you'll have different quality of flour coming into the bakery. You must have bakers that understand how to adjust because you do have to adjust. It really is a combination of finding (and training) the right employees and automation that will lead to winning in the marketplace."[20]

ABA and many of its members are deeply committed to assisting veterans through the hard transition out of the military and into the civilian work force. The industry continues to grow and reinforce a meaningful and highly impactful strategic alliance with the United Services Organization (USO) to proactively recruit veterans into the baking industry.

Erin Sharp is the group vice president of manufacturing at The Kroger Co., one of the largest retailers in the United States. Kroger operates "35 food production or manufacturing facilities producing high quality private-label"[21] bakery, dairy, and other products. Ms. Sharp, too, is a former chair of ABA's board of directors, and the first woman to hold the position in the traditionally male-dominated baking industry.

As a true believer in the power of relationships, Ms. Sharp is a serious champion of:

- **Mentoring**—"I just made a point to never turn down a request to be a mentor. For those of you seasoned leaders, open yourself up to be mentors. Those relationships are absolutely critical for success."[22]
- **Diversity and inclusion**—"You're only as strong as how you represent your customer base, and our customer base is as diverse as

it could be knowing that we serve customers in almost the entire country. And being able to represent our customers with our associates is very, very important to us."[23]

- **Hiring veterans**—"Be patient. It's not an easy transition from military life to business life for many. Create an environment where they can thrive."[24]

Sharp tells a remarkable story of one of their veteran success stories that drives home the importance of focusing on people as individuals worthy of our time and attention, which is a core value for Kroger, ABA, and many of its strategic partners.

The story is about Julia Benitez, a former U.S. Marine Corps major,[25] who made the list of "2016 Top Women in Grocery: Rising Stars."[26] Erin Sharp first met Julia over a phone call that had been scheduled for 15 minutes and ended up lasting two hours. Ms. Sharp remembers starting to recruit just 15 minutes into the call. "It was clear to me that she had leadership that would be very difficult to teach anybody. She led a battalion on the front lines of Afghanistan. For us (and me particularly) it was 'Wow. That's the kind of leadership you can't teach people.' But I can teach someone how to run a plant."[27] Ms. Sharp recalls focusing her transition on "all of the aspects of taking the leadership that she had learned in the military . . . and transition that to running a 150- to 250-member manufacturing plant."[28]

When asked for advice on how to work with veterans, Sharp said, "Understand the individual and what their skills and experiences have been in the military," and then "find the parallels . . . to what you need from them to be successful in whatever leadership role you have in mind for them."[29] And again, be patient.

Sharp, along with other industry leaders, encouraged their partners to expand their reach into the workforce arena. ABA, notes MacKie, "welcomed the opportunity to amplify the baking industry's values and support workforce initiatives as part of the industry's strategic plan."

Through the USO Pathfinder Transition Program and by hosting the effort through the Baking Industry Alliance, the organization engages military service members in worker recruitment events. Crystal Kearns, Senior Transitions Manager, USO acknowledges the industry's values, "What is awesome about the baking industry is that they have a variety of occupations, which is just like the military. Specifically, you have logistics, transportation, mechanics, manufacturers, marketing representatives—the military has all of those as well."[30] An ABA study of frontline workers identified more than 3,000 veterans employed in frontline baking industry careers.

MacKie, in partnership with the board, developed other workforce solutions for new employees on the new worker and existing worker fronts:

- With an uptick in new hires, the industry needed onboarding training support. Designed through the organization's "Bakers Manufacturing Academy's Basics 101 course," new hires are introduced to a wide array of areas that include foundational knowledge, important skills, scope of responsibilities, and behaviors that support wholesale banking operations and procedures. The program is offered in English, Spanish, and Portuguese. ABA is already working toward the next step, opening doors for discussions with community colleges and technical schools to seek adaption of this program in their course offerings.

- Through a Baking Industry's Frontline Workforce Landscape study conducted by ABA and ndp | analytics, entry level workers have ample opportunities to advance their careers. In 2019, the study reported upward mobility for a majority (66 percent) of its workforce: at least one in four frontline supervisors or managers were promoted from within their firms. Pat Richards, vice president, organizational development and recruitment, Hearthside Food Solutions, worked with other industry leaders through ABA to design a baking industry career path. This resource identifies six commercial bakers' paths for industry workers, including production, engineering/equipment maintenance, shipping/distribution, quality assurance/food safety, sanitation, and sales. The career path roadmap, notes Mr. Roberts, "will provide job seekers and current employees with a clear visual of the many opportunities available within the industry"[31]

Sharp represents both Kroger's values and ABA's values. The overlap is not accidental. Successful strategic partnerships begin with relationships that are grounded in shared values and outcomes. The careful reader will have noticed that Fred Penny of Bimbo Bakeries USA, Brad Alexander of Flowers Foods, and Erin Sharp of Kroger each served as chair of the ABA board of directors. And Bill Paterakis of H&S is on ongoing and important industry voice on the board of directors.

Each has close and lasting personal relationships with MacKie, and that has helped ABA's president and CEO stay current on future and evolving challenges facing the industry. And each of the executives has benefitted from a close and vigorous alliance with the baking industry.

Supply Chain Alignment

ABA has been actively pursuing more serious relationships with its supply-chain partner associations in order to better align policy communications. One of the key strategic relationships is the Food and Beverage Industry Alliance that Robb MacKie co-chairs with Alison Bodor, president and CEO, American Frozen Food Institute, and an unofficial steering committee that included Michael Dykes, DVM, president and CEO, International Dairy Foods Association; Leslie Sarasin, president and CEO, FMI - The Food Industry Association; Greg Ferrara, president and CEO, National Grocers Association; and Julie Anna Potts, president and CEO, North American Meat Institute.

This influential alliance helps unite interconnected industries and allows them to stay ahead of impractical and sometimes unacceptable governmental overreach. These partnership efforts are successfully expanding levers of industry influence to shape the challenging and complex business and regulatory environment.

Their ability to impact and shape the environment, especially in a time of crisis, was on full display. Once the global pandemic took hold, regulators from all levels of government sought to lock down every aspect of the economy. Here is where strategic relationships among the food industry mattered. Consumers needed to eat, which meant it was essential to assure the integrity and safety of the food supply chain. MacKie, Ms. Bodor, and the Alliance consolidated resources to make sure families and individuals could eat.

A critical part of this effort was getting the baking industry workers designated as critical infrastructure. Achieving this designation helped the industry keep plants, factories, shipping, logistics, and retail stores open. This is not to say that shielding workers and companies from the pandemic wasn't necessary. It was. The industry partnership also worked with regulators and helped to design effective safety protocols to protect its workers. Afterward, leaders throughout the food industry acknowledged the success of the partnership. One acknowledgement by Nadine Salameh, executive vice president at Bakery de France, reflected a flood of appreciation by the entire industry for helping to keep companies in business.

The Alliance partnership would prove its value again and again. Two bakers approached MacKie with safety concerns. Route sales representatives and merchandisers were in the store at the same time customers were, and it heightened anxiety. He reached out to peers representing the food retailers—Leslie Sarasin at the Food Marketing Institute and Greg Ferrara at the National Grocers Association—and said, "Is there any way that that you all could communicate out to your members to try to move perishable direct store delivery windows to nonbusiness hours? Our bakers will figure out when you just tell them when so that we can cut down on that." Although it took several weeks, the situation improved.

The other area where these partnerships mattered was the food service bakers. They shared with Robb MacKie that they were running out of storage capacity. Working with the Global Cold Chain Alliance, another industry partner, they set up a one-to-one contact between these companies to find capacity.

Throughout the pandemic, the Food and Beverage Issue Alliance (FBIA) acted collaboratively and quickly to keep food supplies maintained for the country's hungry and anxious consumers. Recognizing the importance of the partnership, MacKie proudly proclaimed, "our group of willing participants helped to guide us, and made a significant contribution to the baking industry, the overall food industry, and to our country." These efforts are not limited to the pandemic.

The bakery industry supply chain is an enormous and extremely complex ecosystem consisting of the complete food, beverage, and agriculture industries. In fact, ABA is itself a microcosm of its own supply chain ecosystem in the trade-association universe. Figure 4.2 will give you some idea of the extent of the bakery industry supply chain, but please note it is by no means exhaustive.

Shaping the External Environment, Part 3

One outstanding example of successful collaborative advocacy across the supply chain is the 2021 "Feeding the Economy" study, which was jointly commissioned by 33 food, beverage, and agriculture industry associations working together to shine a light on the monumental, combined impact these industries have on the national economy. The study serves as "a reminder of the critical role that the United States food and agriculture industries . . . play in a resilient food supply chain, fueling our nation and ensuring that Americans are supplied with an abundance of safe food."[32]

The study shows that one-fifth of the nation's economy and one-quarter of American jobs are linked to the food and agriculture sectors, either directly or indirectly. Here are the key findings:

- Total Jobs: 40,714,808
- Total Wages: $2.04 trillion
- Total Taxes: $797.22 billion
- Exports: $155.58 billion
- Total Food and Industry Economic Impact: $6.975 trillion[33]

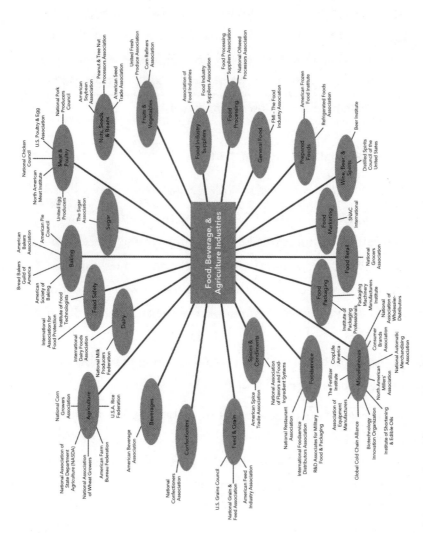

Figure 4.2 The Food, Beverage, and Agriculture Ecosystem

Source: Illustration artwork prepared by Erin Wagner, Edge Research.

Robb MacKie of ABA expressed participants' hope that "policymakers will consider this powerful economic impact as they make key decisions and shape policy." John Bode, president and CEO of the Corn Refiners Association (CRA), echoed the sentiment: "These numbers leave no doubt that food and agriculture remain absolutely central to our nation's well-being . . . This data is essential for policymakers considering changes to tax and trade issues that might affect the food and agriculture sectors."[34]

Shaping the External Environment, Part 4

The U.S. Food and Drug Administration (FDA) produces and enforces food labeling regulations to comply with statutory requirements. Sometimes, it turns out, timetables for compliance are onerous, even impossible. And changes can be expensive.

For a little bit of context, the FDA's *A Food Labeling Guide: Guidance for Industry* is a 130-page document. It covers everything from allowable food names ("When are fanciful names permitted as the statement of identity?") to health claims ("What are the requirements to use the word *healthy*?"); from net quantity of contents to placement on packaging; from ingredients lists ("Should water be listed as an ingredient?") to nutrition labeling ("Is nutrition labeling required for fresh fruit included in a gift package?"). It really is quite an extraordinary document. I point this out to draw attention to the fact that when a requirement changes, packaging must change. And that is not an inconsequential undertaking, especially for a large grocery company that may have more than 20,000 stock-keeping units (SKUs), each of which will need a new package to meet the new requirements.

Erin Sharp faced exactly that scenario at Kroger. The FDA made changes to labeling requirements and included a short timeframe for compliance. After looking at the number of SKUs between their own manufacturing and their suppliers, Ms. Sharp realized that it would not be physically possible to meet the new requirements in the time allotted. There are a limited number of packaging converters, and funneling a huge number of SKUs through those relatively few packaging converters was simply not feasible in the originally too-short timeframe.

MacKie works hard to maintain close relationships with key FDA officials. In fact, he told me that during this particular season of difficulties he talks with a friend at FDA at least twice a day because his friend needs him as a conduit for "real world, real time insight on the ground," which is otherwise lacking. Because of his trusted relationships, MacKie is able to credibly inject the practical implications of these kinds of changes into the conversation.

Working with ABA, Ms. Sharp's team was able to persuade the FDA to grant a reasonable time extension for full compliance.

The extension allowed Kroger to do a relatively soft conversion as opposed to a hard (and expensive) conversion. They were able to make the required packaging changes when they would have normally touched packing anyway for a great number of SKUs. It allowed them "to efficiently and effectively run out packaging, and not waste— from a sustainability standpoint and a financial standpoint—probably well in excess of $100,000 worth of packaging"[35] that they could still utilize and run out.

Ms. Sharp notes that they were not opposed to the changes. The issue was the practicality of getting it done. And being able to go in and share that information in the right way with the FDA is what she believes helped them get the extension. She credits ABA as a significant factor in their successful petition.

In another context, Ms. Sharp had this to say regarding her partnership with ABA:

> As a large organization, we do have some government relations folks in Washington . . . The relationship [with] ABA allows our government relations team to focus on the things that are unique to Kroger, knowing . . . the food manufacturing space, particularly the baking area . . . [is] covered [by] ABA. We've really focused on building the partnership with our government relations team and ABA's team.[36]

Shaping the External Environment, Part 5

Part of the baking industry's success has a lot to do with its selfless approach and willingness to go the extra mile to help others. Board members, ABA staff, and their CEO utilize sincere outreach to expand relationships and then identify opportunities over time to advance the greater good. Robb MacKie serves as chairman of the Council of Manufacturing Associations of the National Association of Manufacturers (NAM). The group represents manufacturing trade associations from all industry sectors and collaborates with Jay Timmons, president and CEO of NAM, and his staff to help enact policy outcomes favorable to all manufacturers. In assuming this role, Robb MacKie unselfishly sees this as strengthening the whole of manufacturing by strengthening the component parts, shaping both the environment and business returns for the industry.

Similar to any other industry nowadays, there must be a return on time and money invested. Since ABA is widely viewed as *The Industry*, the bar for success is unusually high. Thanks in large part to honest communications, transparency, and aligning with industry strategies and outcomes, MacKie and his team are viewed as essential to the industry's future outcomes. ABA's board leadership enthusiastically invests precious time and money. Board meetings make the best use of time as they surface and address current and future challenges that ABA can help address. Conferences deliver real-time business solutions for members and the industry. In many cases, they can be applied immediately.

As an industry trade association, ABA embraces transparency and the importance of communication with the industry. Whether it be direct engagement with company leaders or through its annual report, Robb MacKie and his team communicate ROI throughout the year. This outreach demonstrates quantifiable ROI for the baking industry. Companies see the business impact in their cost of doing business and maintaining capacity to bring current and new products to consumers.

These efforts speak volumes about the importance of honesty and transparency in partnership relationships, and also about the power of commitment and trust when everyone is on the same page. Clearly defining expectations and metrics on the front end and maintaining open and honest communications reflects a strong bond of trust that serves the industry well.

Conclusion

Fred Penny, president and CEO of Bimbo Bakeries USA, reflects the values held by the entire industry: "We've got to be prepared to do the right things. We need to continue to navigate the pandemic, double down on the mission, and do what we need to do on behalf of our customers, associates, and our consumers." In an industry recovering from the global pandemic and experiencing disruption, its pathway forward is clear. Through a robust network of baking industry companies and executives who unite with ABA, its team, and its durable ecosystem, there is a sense of unity and purpose. These characteristics are supported by open and honest communication and transparency.

As automation, omni-channel marketing, workforce challenges, and rapidly changing consumer tastes plague the industry, baker confidence in the future remains unshaken because of the durable community it built through the American Bakers Association. They realize that the durable strategic relationships that are constantly cultivated throughout the supply chain have the baking industry poised to convert challenges to positive business outcomes regardless of any future challenges they might face. It's the right place to be in an ongoing era of uncertainty and disruption.

Even before the global pandemic, Robb MacKie and ABA applied their collaborative and strategic alliance focus to help the industry reduce costs and maintain its competitiveness. While COVID-19, a black swan event, raised the stakes for the baking industry, it relied upon its strategic partner association to unite the supply chain, build out their ecosystem, keep factories open, maintain worker safety, and deliver food to anxious consumers.

Nowadays stakeholders can be as unforgiving as they can be grateful. Executives are mobile: they vote with their feet by leaving and finding return on time and money somewhere else. In the aftermath of COVID-19, industry leaders expect and demand strategic solutions that move the needle on the top line or the bottom line.

Based on performance, the baking industry believes their strategic partner, the ABA, produces quantifiable results. The board and the membership decided to acknowledge their strategic partner. They unanimously supported an increase in their annual financial investment. They affirmed that baking companies and suppliers recognize the role that the ABA plays in shaping a challenging business landscape.

Lest we forget, in a time of national emergency (COVID-19), the baking industry and the strategic partnership built among supply chain partners throughout the food industry associations answered a clarion call. A safe food supply flowed to consumers. Bravo.

5 Unmanned Systems

When I was younger, I was fascinated and delighted by movie and cartoon depictions of a futuristic world filled with flying cars, moving sidewalks, self-driving transit systems, and lots of robots handling all sorts of everyday functions. Almost everything was automated. Some of it struck me as fanciful and even pretty far-fetched. Now I'm not so sure any of it was as unlikely as it seemed not so long ago. The future is upon us. Unmanned systems of every variety are a reality.

Unmanned systems can be defined as the technologies, hardware and software, that do or enable other things to do all manner of tasks either by remote control or automatically with little or no human interaction, intervention, or interference. The number of things that fall into this category is already immense, and growing rapidly and continuously. The impact of unmanned systems on everyday life is as vast as it is disruptive. And it looks for all the world like it's here to stay.

The World of Unmanned Systems

The variety of unmanned systems ideas and thinking, technologies and applications, current and future, in many ways defies a coherent taxonomy because so many disparate components overlap and intertwine in ways that are hard to label. There are, nevertheless, some general buckets that will serve our purposes as we begin to make sense of the unmanned systems ecosystem.

First, though, let's get a sense of the community that inhabits and sustains the unmanned systems ecosystem.

The Unmanned Systems Community

The unmanned systems community (see Figure 5.1) is an ever-expanding and ever more consequential sector of the international economy.

Figure 5.1 The Unmanned Systems Community
Source: Illustration artwork prepared by Erin Wagner, Edge Research.

Astonishingly complex and rapidly evolving technology requires broad cooperation and collaboration and highly disciplined strategic thinking, planning, and decision-making in this extraordinary world of interconnected, interdependent, sometimes interlocked cutting-edge technical knowledge and application. It is not for the faint of heart.

You'll note immediately that I have used the word *community* rather than *industry*. It would needlessly oversimplify the reality to speak of an unmanned systems industry. More than 25 discrete industrial sectors of the world's economy are already inextricably linked to the future of unmanned systems. And there are some of those (and many other industries, I suspect) that are not even fully aware of the fact yet. It really is a community held together by mutual interests, a shared vision, and the need for each other to achieve the overall goal of changing the way people and goods are moved.

The unmanned systems community consists of a host of individuals, corporations, and government entities: creators, builders, and users. The assortment of individuals who actively participate in the community is mind boggling, including scientists, researchers, and academicians; officials at all levels of local, state, federal, and international governments and the military; titans of industry and their representatives; even hobbyists and weekend enthusiasts. Organizations that are immersed in the community are from the military-industrial complex, the medical-industrial complex, universities and think tanks, government agencies (again local, state, federal, and international), logistics, package delivery, and transportation companies, and so on.

Unmanned systems have seemingly unlimited practical applications in the defense (military), civil (nonmilitary government entities, including public safety), and commercial markets.

Unmanned Vehicles

Let us start by exploring unmanned vehicles. As with more traditional human-operated vehicles, there are three general domains that most remotely operated, autonomous, and semi-autonomous vehicles fit into, although just as with more traditional human-operated vehicles, there is some overlap: air, land, and sea.

In the Air

Unmanned air/aircraft systems (UAS). The UAS global market is currently $11.3 billion.[1] If you are searching on the Internet, "drones" and "UAVs" (unmanned aerial vehicles) will return many of the results that you are probably seeking. If you are speaking to international (or non-English-speaking national) aviation agencies, use the acronym RPAS (remotely piloted aircraft system). In the United States, call it UAS (unmanned air/aircraft system) if you want to be understood.[2]

Unmanned aerial vehicles are already being used regularly and effectively by the military overseas for such diverse missions as surveillance, mapping, targeting, and destruction of targets. Drones can and do carry cameras, infrared capabilities, and GPS; they also can and do carry and expend rockets, missiles, and bombs. Civilian first responders are experimenting with a wide array of public safety and public health applications. Commercial entities are researching, developing, and testing a broad swath of applications from last mile delivery to private transportation. The FAA projects the commercial small unmanned aircraft systems (UAS) sector will more than double by 2024, growing from 385,000 commercial drones at the end of 2019 to 828,000.[3]

Some top companies in the air domain include Boeing, PAR-ROT, Titan Aerospace, AAI, Northrop Grumman, IAI, Dynali helicopters, BAE Systems, and SAGEM.[4]

On Land (Ground)

Unmanned ground vehicle (UGV). Like UAVs, UGVs have a plethora of current and future military, civil, and commercial applications. Although in the recent past the market was dominated by military research, development, experimentation, and deployment (primarily for search and rescue missions, explosive ordnance disposal, and combat support), civil and commercial markets are expanding rapidly. The oil and gas industries, for example, are pursuing applications for exploration and recovery. The agricultural robots market is forecasted to grow from $7.4 billion in 2020 to $20.6 billion by 2025.[5] New manufacturing applications are regularly being tested and deployed.

And almost everyone everywhere is looking for new and improved transportation solutions, not just a few of whom are looking forward to a world of fully automated, autopiloted commercial and personal passenger and delivery trains, long-haul trucks, buses, cars, SUVs, vans, even recreational vehicles. There is literally no form of transportation that is off the discussion table.

Some major companies in the ground domain include Armtrac Limited, Clearpath Robotics, Inc., Cobham plc, DOK-ING, Endeavor Robotics, General Dynamics Corporation, Horiba Mira Ltd., Icor Technology, Northrop Grumman Corporation, QinetiQ Group plc, RE2, Inc., Lockheed Martin, Oshkosh Corporation, BAE Systems, iRobot Corp., FLIR Systems, Milrem AS, Textron Systems, Howe & Howe Technologies, Inc., and L3Harris Technologies.[6]

And Sea (Maritime)

Unmanned surface vehicle (USV) (or autonomous surface vehicle [ASV]) and unmanned underwater vehicle (UUV). The global USV market was valued at $1.5 billion in 2019 and is expected to reach $3.1 billion by 2025.[7] "Experts project the unmanned underwater vehicles (UUV) global market to hit the $5.2 billion dollar mark by 2022. This is largely due to increasing demands for commercial subsea construction-related applications, including surveys, seabed mapping, and pipeline inspections."[8] Current military applications include sea mine detection and clearing, submarine hunting and tracking, and general maritime situational awareness.

USVs and ASVs are currently operating on the rather murky fringes of international maritime law, which has a great deal of regulatory catching up to do with regard to capabilities and uses.

A few of the prominent companies in the USV/UUV space include Liquid Robotics, Inc., Teledyne Technologies, Inc., Rafael Advanced Defense Systems, Atlas Elektronik, ECA Group, ASV Global, XOCEAN, 5G International, Inc., SeaRobotics, Elbit Systems, and Textron, Inc.[9]

Crossovers and Outliers

There are other unmanned vehicles that should be mentioned before we move on. They don't quite fit neatly into any of the three primary domains, but they do represent cutting-edge technology. There are unmanned maritime surface vehicles that can crawl out of the water and drive away on land. Of course, their counterparts in the world of manned vehicles have existed for a long time. One thinks of military troop landing craft going back to World War II, and perhaps of

Duck Tours. There are drones that can land on water and skim along the surface or dive beneath the waves. Versions of that technology, too, have existed in the manned vehicle world for years. Think of seaplanes. There are unmanned submarines that can come blasting out of the water and take flight.

Too, there are unmanned space vehicles ranging from NASA's renowned Mars rover *Perseverance* (a UGV, but developed for ground other than Earth), to the Hubble Space Telescope, to all manner of satellites (UAVs, but designed for orbit outside our atmosphere). More recently, drones took to the skies over Mars as the first aircraft to do so. When a small helicopter named *Ingenuity* took off from the surface of Mars, it made history as the first aircraft to fly in the atmosphere of another planet. The drone initially landed on Mars inside the NASA rover *Perseverance* on February 18, 2021.

I will not be surprised if new domains or categories of unmanned vehicles emerge in the not-too-distant future, but for now suffice it to say that unmanned vehicles are just one piece of the large and complex unmanned systems ecosystem (see Figure 5.2). And like all ecosystems, each constituent is integral to the whole and all are interdependent.

Note: There are approximately 50 major suppliers and manufacturers of unmanned and autonomous vehicles, systems, and platforms. There are more than 100 suppliers of components for unmanned systems (UAVs/drones, UGVs, surface vessels, and underwater robotics). About 25 key companies supply software developed for the unmanned market, including operating systems; data correction, analysis, and processing; and mapping software. And there are about 60 major suppliers of services within the unmanned systems industry.

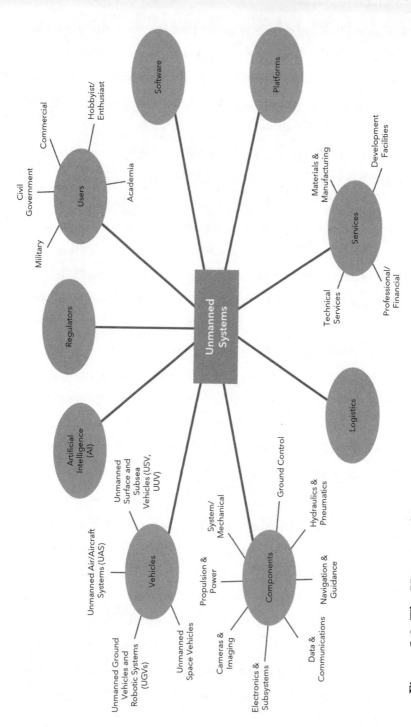

Figure 5.2 The Unmanned Systems Ecosystem
Source: Illustration artwork prepared by Erin Wagner, Edge Research.

As you can see from the illustration, the unmanned systems eco-system comprises a wide range of occasionally surprising and I would have said unexpected constituents. Note the inclusion of regulators and users, software and hardware (vehicle components), vehicles and platforms, artificial intelligence, services, and logistics. At first glance, one might be reminded of the old *Sesame Street* song, "One of These Things Is Not Like the Others." Indeed, several of these things are not like the others, and several of the interrelationships appear tenu-ous at best. And yet they do in fact make up an inescapable, interde-pendent whole.

Each constituent of this ecosystem deserves far more attention than we have space for here. In fact, excellent books have been written on the science behind the astonishing technologies represented just by the vehicle components, let alone the frontiers of artificial intel-ligence and robotics. The work that is being done in the fields of data and communications, propulsion and power, cameras and imaging, navigation and guidance, and all the rest reads like science fiction. We will therefore not take the time to explore all these constituents individually, except insofar as they might further our understanding of how strategic partnerships can protect, sustain, and grow dynamic (and often fragile) ecosystems.

Association for Unmanned Vehicle Systems International (AUVSI)

AUVSI is "the world's largest nonprofit association devoted exclu-sively to unmanned systems and robotics,"[10] counting among its more than 7,500 members some 600 corporate members (from more than 60 countries) and a diverse array of partner organizations, as well as individual enthusiasts from the military, civil service, academia, and private citizenry. Members include not only some of the largest capitalized companies on the planet but also some start-ups and everything in between—just like the ecosystem itself.

The majority of members are thoroughly persuaded that all of the constituents that make up the unmanned systems ecosystem must work together in order to move unmanned systems forward into the future. Many are convinced that collaboration is not only a good thing but a necessary thing for the ecosystem to flourish. It doesn't hurt that many of them have experienced the benefits of cross-pollinating ideas for pushing innovation and recognize the power of cooperation not only to expand horizons intellectually, scientifically, and technologically but also to broaden public appeal, build trust, and encourage acceptance across the board.

AUVSI is aiming to "create a future in which remotely operated and autonomous transportation technologies are fully accepted, valued, and used to move people, things, and data safely and efficiently . . . AUVSI serves as the industry focal point to connect, convene, communicate, and collaborate with the creators, users, and regulators of this technology to build solutions, regulate their use appropriately, and articulate their utility and value . . . AUVSI is committed to fostering the growth, long-term viability and stability of the unmanned systems industry, and works to unify the industry across domains to advance how the world embraces unmanned and autonomous systems technologies."[11]

In other words, AUVSI regards itself as both the manifestation and the champion of all things unmanned; and its members, a microcosm of the ecosystem, agree and accept it as such. Thus AUVSI, their strategic and data-driven partner, was chosen de facto to collect and analyze industry intelligence from across the full community and develop a strategic plan to move the entire system forward.

AUVSI president and CEO Brian Wynne is a keen-minded, stout-hearted, Jesuit-trained man of unyielding honesty, determination, integrity, courage, and action. He is also a licensed commercial pilot who flies his own airplane. He and his dedicated board and team at the association are executing a data-driven strategic plan that is effectively steering and advancing the industry through rapid growth and no small amount of ambiguity into what they hope will be a bright, clear future.

The Strategic Plan

According to the data gleaned from surveying a broad swath of industry professionals including members, nonmembers, and representatives across all technology domains, the number one uncertainty challenge (and therefore the number one priority focus) for the unmanned systems community is public awareness and acceptance. That is their core issue.

Dr. Cara LaPointe, co-director of the John's Hopkins Institute for Assured Autonomy, agrees with that assessment. Referencing a talk she gave on the subject of assured autonomy, AUVSI stated: "As with any emerging technology, unmanned and autonomous systems must demonstrate that they can reliably perform the operations for which they are designed. The stakes for the unmanned industry are high: If society does not trust the technology, its immense benefits will not be realized."[12]

Dr. LaPointe recommended a holistic approach toward assured autonomy predicated on these three points:

1. The system must be safe, reliable, secure, and resilient.

2. The unmanned ecosystem must be seamlessly integrated across networks and domains.

3. Public policy must support autonomous systems that are ethical and beneficial to society.[13]

And that is why two of AUVSI's most important strategic goals (at least for the purposes of our discussion) are designed largely to promote a positive industry image and ensure that unmanned and autonomous systems are widely embraced for the value they create. These goals are to:

1. Educate citizens, elected officials, regulators, and the media on the benefits and safety of unmanned and autonomous systems.

2. Advocate for the establishment of laws and regulations that enable the development and expanded operation of unmanned systems.[14]

The Decision Matrix

When explaining his rationale and game plan for tackling public acceptance as the biggest barrier to the success of unmanned systems and therefore the primary challenge, Brian Wynne referenced an old college friend of his named Chris McGoff, who wrote a book called *The Primes: How Any Group Can Solve Any Problem*. In this book, McGoff describes a matrix with Social Complexity on the *x*-axis and

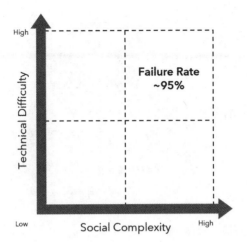

Figure 5.3 Quad 4
Source: Illustration artwork prepared by Erin Wagner, Edge Research.

Technical Difficulty on the *y*-axis, and describes "Quad 4" (the top right quadrant) as the realm of highest risk and highest impact. That is where the vast majority of efforts fail. See Figure 5.3.

In a TED Talk on the subject, McGoff suggested that the people who tend to thrive in Quad 4 do so because they have moral courage, a term he attributed to the late Rushworth Kidder. According to Kidder, moral courage requires "the recognition of risk, and willingness to endure . . . in the service of principle."[15] McGoff agreed with the idea that moral courage exists where danger, endurance, and principles meet. See Figure 5.4.

He then went on to say, "What the winners do is they bring forward a piece of vision that is like a piece of Swiss cheese. It's delicious in what it says, but there are these gaping holes . . . And people say, 'Well, what about this and what about that?' The people who thrive in Quad 4 have the guts to say: 'I don't know that. Can you help me?' And you know what the world says? 'Oh yeah. I've got ideas

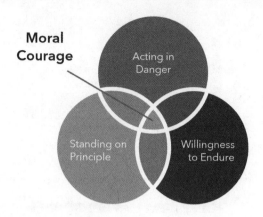

Figure 5.4 Moral Courage
Source: Illustration artwork prepared by Erin Wagner, Edge Research.

about that. Let me co-create that with you.'"[16] That is the approach
that Brian Wynne and AUVSI are taking. Deliberately. Mr. Wynne
recognizes the difficulty of the task; he is alive to the risk, but he
is willing to endure because he believes that what they are doing is
right and good. He's going all in, as he puts it, on "the fewest most
important things" that they can and will "do everything about."

With regard to living and breathing in Quad 4 the whole time,
Mr. Wynne admits that there is a high degree of technical difficulty,
but he is quite confident that all of the technical difficulties can be
solved over time. Social complexity is the long pole in the tent. There
are a lot of things that can go wrong. Because all of the technological
advances and testing and experimentation are being done on a multi-
domain basis, there are all kinds of public concerns about privacy,
safety, and so on. In order to have a scalable market, people need to
accept the technologies. And to do that, they must trust them.

One thing Wynne is quite certain about is that they cannot afford
to underestimate the social complexity. They need to try to address

the fears and concerns both of the regulators and of the average citizen up front. Honesty, openness, transparency; these are what are needed. And it's being accomplished.

Before we look at how that's being done, let's take a moment to consider Brian Wynne's thinking with regard to the unmanned systems community and AUVSI's overall role and approach to representing the community's interests.

Engaging All the Aspects of the Value Chain

When speaking of the unmanned systems ecosystem, Mr. Wynne is careful to differentiate between the supply chain and what he calls the value chain. As an economist by training, he deeply understands the supply chain and how important it is. So much so, in fact, that he considers Martin Van Creveld's *Supplying War: Logistics from Wallenstein to Patton* to be probably one of the most important books he's ever read in his life. In the world of technology, however, it is all about the value chain. The great challenge is to take the extremely "disparate interests that are coming together to make this socially complex, technically difficult thing a reality, and channel them all in the same direction."

AUVSI has an extraordinarily diverse membership today—far more so than before. It did not happen by accident. The move to expand and diversify was very intentional. And as long as Brian Wynne has anything to say about it, it will continue to get broader and more diverse, by design. Prior to his arrival at AUVSI, Wynne recalls that "there were some folks (in local governments, for example) that had been opposed and even hostile to the idea of unmanned systems in general, in any domain, but particularly things flying over their heads that they don't have any control over. Now these same folks are embracing the technology, and they're now joining the association." Again, it's not by accident.

Although AUVSI is still an industrial trade association, Wynne also sees it as "a platform where all of the different members of that value chain can come together and partner with each other a little bit more directly. And everything we do is really informed by that concept and that approach."

A Vision for Unmanned Systems

To best capture Brian Wynne's vision, I am including his own words from a speech welcoming participants and guests to AUVSI's flagship conference XPONENTIAL 2021:

> What I have realized is that accelerating along this continuum depends largely on our preparedness to holistically support the safe and seamless integration of these systems. If we want to ensure unmanned systems continue to be a force for good, we must promote advancement and integration in a way that is sustainable and earns the trust of regulators and the public.
>
> I'd like to suggest three considerations that will be key to our medium- and long-term success: partnerships within the user communities, collaboration with regulators (indeed, government officials at all levels), and industry cohesion.
>
> First, in prioritizing safe integration we recognize that the development of new technology does not occur in a vacuum. End users often have their own safety standards and requirements, which is how they maintain the public trust. Major industries are leveraging

unmanned systems to improve their safety records, a process we can build upon to everyone's benefit . . .

Second, we must continue to work in lockstep with regulators to support a framework that enables a wide range of appropriate use of unmanned systems. AUVSI is working to foster industry/government collaboration, and we've seen success in the last year on the promulgation of regulations that support our industry . . .

Third, as innovation progresses it is absolutely critical that our industry works together to address challenges that exist now and the new ones that will inevitably arise. Our messaging needs to be consistent and forward-leaning. We can be competitive with each other, sure. That's just business. But common cause requires that we rise above parochial interests to achieve what would advance the agenda for our entire community . . . we can all be proud of what we have achieved by defining and striving toward collective goals. Industry cohesion is not easy to achieve, particularly when technology leads us into uncharted waters.[17]

Strategic Collaboration

An outside study commissioned by Mr. Wynne concluded that "AUVSI is leveraging the industry, utilizing critical mass, to accelerate acceptance of unmanned technology . . . What really matters is how it's all about the industry and not one company."[18] Interestingly, the study also confirmed that the single most important CEO strength in the industry—as identified by a survey of industry CEOs—is what was described as Effective Collaborator. Brian Wynne put it like this: "Our industry will succeed together if we address technology, ecosystem, and policy challenges through a collaborative process. We will have our differences, but with safety as our lodestar we will achieve the most success when we work together, collaborate with lawmakers and regulators, and educate end users and the public."

The centerpiece of AUVSI's strategy to ensure safety and public acceptance is strategic collaboration, which sits at the confluence of relationship supremacy (especially alignment on values and outcomes and honest communications and trust) and business dominance (especially strategic thinking and focus on data and analytics).

Civil Government Collaboration

Public Safety

Brian Wynne's favorite community that is rapidly adopting the use of UAS is the public safety community. From his frame of reference, that is a big deal because as an economist he usually would put logistics first. Public safety is a varied community; it includes firefighters, emergency responders, police, search-and-rescue workers, and more. When I asked him why he is particularly drawn to that community, his response was telling: "They're public safety. And the most important thing to our success as a community is public acceptance. And the number one concern of the public is safety: are these systems safe?"

He elaborated further: "What better approach could one have than to support the public safety community, while they are demonstrating that this is technology that we can use to find people faster, this is technology that we can use to respond to disasters, this is technology that we can use to deliver vaccines to places that are very difficult to reach, or otherwise keep people at social distance. You get the idea."

There are a number of ways that unmanned systems are being utilized in law enforcement. Just as in the military, unmanned systems can provide all sorts of tools for greater situational awareness. But from a strictly public safety perspective, the classic example of how these new technologies can be used to protect and serve is being demonstrated in Chula Vista, California.

Mr. Wynne told me the tale:

The Chula Vista Police Department has been using a fairly sophisticated drone, sending it out in advance of the squad car, arriving on-scene for whatever kind of fracas might be underway, or suspicious behavior, or this, that, and the other thing.

In one instance, there was a report of someone waving a gun around in front of a fast-food restaurant. The drone was dispatched and arrived before the squad car. The drone operator, who was watching the drone footage in real time, saw the individual waving something around that looked like a gun. But at some point, the operator realized that the man was lighting his cigarette with this device.

Now, you can imagine the difference in response between these two possible reports: (1) "We have an individual acting strangely. He has something in his hand. It's a cigarette lighter" versus (2) "We have an individual acting strangely. He has a gun in his hand." The police responding in the squad car showed up with solid, verified information. They were much calmer and more controlled than they might have been otherwise. As a result, they didn't overreact to a situation that with vague or incorrect information could have ended tragically.

What made the Chula Vista program stand out in Wynne's mind was the public education that they did in advance of flying the drone the first time. People were prepared and were thus not surprised or alarmed by its presence. They understood that it was a tool used by their local law enforcement to keep them safe and minimize mistakes or overreactions. The increased situational awareness has allowed cops to arrive peacefully on a number of scenes where a person may have been disturbed or upset in some way, but not a threat. And the police have been able to resolve these potentially tense situations in a good and proper order.

Law Enforcement

Another use for drones that has been highly effective where it's been tested is in the aftermath of a car accident. Car accidents are notorious for disrupting the lives (or at least the schedules) of innocent passersby. A bad accident, for example, will require a police report. This often involves studying the scene of an accident in minute detail, taking photographs, measuring skid marks, and so forth. These kinds of mechanical tasks can be done on the scene in a fraction of the time and with minimal obstruction of traffic by drones. Moreover, it's inherently dangerous for officers to be walking around in traffic. Drones can dramatically reduce the time that a road or lanes on a highway are out of service due to accident report activity, and they can also minimize danger to police and even other drivers who get distracted in heavy traffic.

According to Mr. Wynne, "in every single instance where law enforcement is utilizing unmanned systems, the success of the mission is almost entirely a function of how well they communicate about it.

It is vital that law enforcement mitigate potential misunderstanding and negative reaction as much as possible. The public needs to know, for example, when a police department deploys a drone in the evening that it is not being used for surveillance, but rather that it is being sent out to find an elderly Alzheimer's patient who has wandered off. There have been many instances of people being found much faster by drones, particularly at night when time is of the essence.

"Communicating in advance," Mr. Wynne says, "is the difference between that tool being available in the public safety toolbox or that tool being viewed with inherent suspicion and therefore disallowed."

Federal Aviation Administration (FAA)

AUVSI has been working hand in glove with the FAA for some time now, and the partnership has been a boon to both parties. The truth is that it's an important strategic partnership. Of course, there are many associations that cooperate with and have excellent relationships with the regulatory agencies that oversee their business functions. But AUVSI's partnership with the FAA is intentional.

Brian Wynne notes that "when the introduction of a new technology needs to be encouraged by policy or enabled by regulatory action, it is incumbent upon industry to bring the solutions forward. We can't expect our regulators to know what the right way to regulate the industry is unless we tell them what the industry is capable of." Technology obviously advances much faster than the regulations that govern it. By law, regulations are deliberative and can only be implemented after a significant cost analysis is completed. In Mr. Wynne's estimation, "the industry has to bring the regulator along. The burden is really increasingly on industry."

Mr. Wynne explained to me what he meant:

> In the unmanned systems air domain this is on steroids because
> there's literally no predicate for what we're doing with unmanned
> systems. The entire aviation regulatory system is built on one pilot,
> one aircraft, seeing and avoiding other aircraft. We don't have
> pilots on these aircraft; therefore pilots cannot see and avoid other
> aircraft. So we have to build an entirely new regulatory structure
> based around new detect and avoid technology.
>
> The other thing that is very different in a technology context—and
> the FAA has been moving in this direction to great benefit in the
> airspace—is rather than a regulator prescribing what needs to be
> done in order for a pilot or an aircraft or an operation to be com-
> pliant with regulations, they have been moving to performance-
> based regulations. So rather than saying, "Here's your widget. It
> needs to be like this" (the prescriptive regulation), they say "Here's
> what your widget needs to be able to do in this particular environ-
> ment. So if you, Mr. Industry, can prove that it can do that, then
> you can fly."
>
> Now, that's really important because prescriptive regulations can't
> be future-proofed. The technology keeps getting better. And as
> long as we have performance standards that we're playing to, we
> can get better and better and better at how we address and meet
> those performance standards. And those performance standards in
> the airspace are exceedingly high because we don't tolerate conflict
> in the airspace. That's how we maintain such a high level of safety.
> We still have aircraft that run into each other, but it's not as com-
> mon as it once was.

What we're doing is very different. And this partnership is exceedingly important because the industry must be able to engage with the FAA and the FAA must welcome that engagement in order to get this done. Congress has mandated that they integrate unmanned systems into the airspace. That's the law. But we need to help them do that. So there has to be a collaborative dialogue back and forth.

The ultimate goal of commercial unmanned systems is full integration with traditional aviation. Currently, most of the FAA regulations require that unmanned systems remain within visual line of sight: one pilot, one aircraft, see and avoid. The next level, which some describe as the holy grail of commercial unmanned flight, is unmanned systems flying beyond visual line of sight. The military already does this all the time, and does it very well. The technology exists. But from a safety standpoint in the world of civil aircraft there is a lot still to be worked out. Integration becomes a high-stakes game. It will affect every member of the flying public.

Integration is more than just accommodating unmanned systems in the airspace; it means actually integrating them with manned systems. The truth is that more and more things are being automated and will continue to be automated. The trend is upward, with no sign of flattening. UAVs flying over the horizon is just the next step. The automation of things will eventually include the air traffic control systems and everything else related to safety in the skies. It will take time, but it does seem at this point to be inexorable. Until full integration happens, it is critical that testing and experimentation do not degrade the safety of the airspace. In the end, automation should actually improve the safety of the airspace. And it should improve efficiency, which would not go unnoticed.

One of the more visible collaborative efforts of the strategic partnership between the FAA and AUVSI is called the FAA UAS symposium, which is now in its fifth year. This is the only event I'm aware of that is co-hosted by a regulatory agency and the industry it represents, with the stated purpose of helping the regulator bring information out to industry and then have a collaborative dialogue.

That is the purpose of the FAA UAS symposium. Brian Wynne said yes to that arrangement with almost no idea what he was getting AUVSI into. As he remembers it, his second call was to his executive vice president (EVP). He apparently opened that call with "I'm sorry, but we're going to have to figure this out." But the symposium has been extremely valuable to the unmanned systems community and also valuable to AUVSI as an organization, because it really puts them in a unique position to manage and channel certain topics.

The dialogue between the industry and the FAA was not always so collaborative. Mr. Wynne recalls that at the end of his first meeting with then FAA administrator Michael Huerta in 2015, the regulator shook his hand and said, "I hope every discussion that we have is as cordial as this one." Mr. Wynne responded, "I don't know why they wouldn't be." He notes that Mr. Huerta "clearly had a slightly different expectation," possibly even assuming Mr. Wynne would be somewhat confrontational. Mr. Wynne reassured him. "I'm here to partner with you," he said. "Industry is here to partner with you."

Mr. Huerta and subsequent FAA Administrators started attending AUVSI's major trade show every year after that and started making regulatory announcements from their stage. And the relationship has continued.

Mr. Wynne sums up the symbiosis rather tidily:

> Being clear that industry can't regulate, we must collaborate with our regulators. They are by law the ones that set the rules. But they can't do it in a vacuum, and we can't expect them to do it in a vacuum and get it right. And they know it.
>
> So that to me is a critical partnership. I'm sure there are instances where industry and regulators are at odds with one another, and I'm not saying it's all simple and everyone agrees around the tables that we convene either, but to me it is vastly more beneficial to the advancement of the technology and the gleaning of the societal benefits that this technology can bring to have a collaborative relationship between industry and government, industry and regulator, than not.

Commercial Collaboration

Logistics and the Last Mile

AUVSI fosters many partnerships with communities and vertical industries that utilize unmanned systems technology. In some instances, there is an intermingling between those that are in the community and advancing the technology, and those who use it. AUVSI recognizes the importance and vitality of strategic partnerships and therefore not only develops them with many of its own members, but also promotes and encourages them within the community, among members. And perhaps more importantly, AUVSI continues to actively expand the community. AUVSI serves as a broker of relationships.

The logistics community is a good example. As I mentioned, Brian Wynne is a fan of logistics. He told me, "in the instance of every single technology that I've promoted in my career, you know it's for real when the logistics guys show up, because they are serious about efficiency, they are serious about technology, and they have scale. Think about UPS, FedEx, or Purolator for example. They are all recognizing that this technology can be used for everything from last mile deliveries down a dirt path or a gravel road in Montana to Boeing-size cargo aircraft that will not require pilots."

Massive unmanned cargo aircraft are further out, but in late 2013, Amazon CEO Jeff Bezos got the last mile delivery ball rolling in a *60 Minutes* interview where he announced Amazon Prime Air and his plan to deliver packages within an hour. That vision, while not yet fully realized, is making progress. It's a good example of a vertical industry that AUVSI has brought into the fold and leveraged quite significantly.

National Highway Transportation Safety Administration (NHTSA)

AUVSI, and particularly the logistics community within its ranks, is also working with another of its regulators, the NHTSA, to advance integration issues in the ground domain. Together they are seeking to "ensure the agency's automated driving system framework safely integrates automated vehicles into our transportation systems in a way that enables environmental, economic, and workforce benefits of these systems."[19]

Mr. Wynne described some of the common interests and areas for close collaboration that matter most to AUVSI and the NHTSA:

> Anyone who has driven in downtown Washington, DC (or any other big city) will be familiar with the problem of delivery trucks blocking a left lane or a right lane on a busy street. That issue may not necessarily ever go away completely, but the delivery truck might very soon be giving way to sidewalk robots that are delivering those packages. And those sidewalk robots might come out of the back of a delivery truck that hopefully is not double parked in the middle of rush-hour traffic.
>
> That's a simple example of an efficiency that's coming. And we're starting to see it already. But I think a better way of capturing the societal benefit and value would be to consider what's coming out of the tailpipe of that truck. It's gratifying to see Amazon making an announcement that they're going to buy a hundred thousand electrified trucks. That's good for the environment. The studies continue to bear out that even if you're using pulverized coal to make electricity, it's still easier to capture that pollution at a single source than at all the different tailpipe sources that are out there when you're burning gasoline.
>
> Unmanned electric vehicles are making the grid cleaner. And it keeps getting cleaner all the time, very much because of economics as well as climate concerns. And it's hard to overestimate the potential impact of taking vehicles off the road by utilizing the space that's right above our heads more efficiently. It will make cities more livable (and more drivable, if you have to be driving), et cetera. These are things that we have to get to scale to truly realize the benefit from them, but inexorably we will.

Logistics During the Pandemic

The value of AUVSI's commitment to strategic collaboration as the centerpiece of its approach to building a strong and vibrant unmanned systems community and thereby benefiting society as a whole was clearly evident during the COVID-19 pandemic. Brian Wynne touched on it nicely in his opening speech at XPONENTIAL 2021:

> We are reconvening our community after the most challenging year that some of us have ever had to endure; a year that was at the same time full of inspiration and during which we achieved tremendous progress.
>
> In the midst of the Covid health situation a worldwide audience witnessed how rapidly our technology could be deployed for the benefit of society. Unmanned systems technology provided and continues to provide the logistics needed to maintain social distancing while ensuring critical goods are transported to where they are needed most.
>
> Unmanned systems were able to rapidly disinfect public areas and deliver medical supplies like protective gear, PCR tests, and vaccines while limiting human to human exposure. The progress we have made . . . has not only been in response to community needs. We have also continued to address economic and other imperatives. Unmanned systems are increasingly the tools relied on by public safety departments to conduct rescue operations, by utility companies to rapidly return cities to power after natural disasters, and by our military to maintain competitiveness . . . In short, as new logistical challenges have arisen, the unmanned systems community has answered the call and the world has taken note.[20]

Unmanned Systems and Robotics Database

In the spirit of encouraging openness, cross-pollination, and coop-eration, AUVSI developed the largest comprehensive and searchable database of all unmanned vehicles and robotic products operating in the air, ground, and maritime domains. It provides up-to-date, detailed information on unmanned vehicles and robotic products data spanning civil, commercial, and military markets. It is a real-time representation of the value chain and one important way that AUVSI pieces it together.

The Unmanned Systems and Robotics Database has been a tre-mendous resource for connecting individuals, companies, government agencies, and the military with the products and services that they need or think they may need for their work. By connecting thus, they are connecting with one another, and that, too, has created opportu-nities for collaboration and cross-pollination.

According to its website, some of the ways AUVSI's members (and nonmembers) are using the Unmanned Systems and Robotics Database include:

- Agriculture, the oil and gas industries, and even university robot-ics programs explore existing platforms, leading to innovation.

- Law enforcement and first responders determine available plat-forms that meet their application requirements without going through the costly RFP process.

- Manufacturers stay informed of any new product releases, com-petitor platforms, and emerging prototypes. Information is added to the Unmanned Systems and Robotics Database daily so you can be sure you are always kept up-to-date.

- New business partners, potential customers, or acquisition inter-ests are visible to payload developers, startups, and larger manu-facturers interested in expanding their product offerings.

- Operators looking for market-ready products find the best systems to fit their application requirements through advanced search functions.

- Researchers, educators, and analysts assess past, current, emerging, and future capabilities of unmanned systems. The Unmanned Systems and Robotics Database offers unrivaled potential to develop comprehensive market studies.

- Others working in manned or unmanned flight can search for market-ready products that meet size and performance requirements.[21]

Wrapping Up

You may recall a reference to Brian Wynne and his Jesuit training. Students trained at Jesuit institutions understand the value of the education provided. One of the key values is solidarity and kinship. These values shine brightly in Wynne's thoughts and actions. As one thinks of the magnitude of the task facing unmanned systems, it is important to recognize Mr. Wynne's comfort working in a commu-nity setting. This is Mr. Wynne's path forward as the community and AUVSI work to achieve public acceptance.

Brian Wynne and AUVSI are thoroughly committed to cham-pioning honesty, integrity, and transparency as they seek to integrate unmanned systems into the mainstream of modern society. They are thoroughly committed to open dialogue, cooperation, collaboration, and strategic partnerships across the unmanned systems community and beyond to create a safe and beneficial and (largely) automated future society.

As with any new technologies, many people have many questions. Given today's political climate, I asked Mr. Wynne whether the expansion of regulatory authority and regulatory influence over the past two decades might be related to political considerations. Here's what he said:

> Happily, this is not a partisan issue as far as I can tell. And if I have anything to say about it, it won't be a partisan issue. There's literally no purchase in having it become partisan. Partisan in today's parlance equals gridlock in my opinion, not advancement. I'm in Washington to get things done. And I have always looked for opportunities where there is good appreciation on both sides of the aisle. And I've never had any interest in pursuing a particular opportunity if it wasn't bipartisan, if it couldn't be articulated how it benefited everyone across the political spectrum.
>
> Now, that is not to say that there aren't political implications to what we're doing. That is not to say that there won't be potential unintended consequences. There are lots and lots of ethical issues that come into play around artificial intelligence, around cyber security, around how do we query why a machine decided to do what it decided to do, and who's responsible? So, I'm not saying that there aren't political questions that underpin a lot of the things that were doing. But again, the approach to this is to get those out on the table and to look at them. If we can agree on what we are solving for, there's a greater chance that we will keep up with the potential of advancing technology and harness its benefits.

The theme for our most recent event is assured autonomy. No one's going to get in a vehicle without a steering wheel and pedals if it can be hacked. The public will not accept things flying around if we don't have some sense of the fidelity of that system and the reliability that the machine's going to do what it is that we expect it to do. There have been some significant mistakes made in the past under the rubric of permissionless innovation. I'm challenging our community to not repeat those mistakes.

May it be so.

6 Asphalt Pavement

Asphalt is an amazing substance, albeit unsung and taken for granted. When it is combined with stone and gravel (i.e., aggregates) to construct pavements, every American enjoys the benefits of asphalt nearly every single day. There are almost 2.8 million miles of paved roads in the United States, and most of them—about 94 percent—have an asphalt surface.[1] Most of us who live in towns or cities drive on asphalt pavements the moment we pull out of our driveways. We ride on asphalt when we take a taxi, or a bus, or an airplane for that matter (approximately 80 percent of the nearly 3,330 runways in our national airport system are surfaced with asphalt pavement).[2] And nearly everything tangible we buy, use, or consume, at some point traveled on asphalt roads to get to where we could buy, use, or consume it.

Asphalt occurs naturally. Also known as bitumen, it is found in asphalt lakes as a sticky, almost liquid version of "black gold" that can be lightly refined for use in asphalt applications. Asphalt is also found in an almost solid state as a binder in asphalt rocks. It has been used for millennia. The word asphalt is derived from the Greek *asphaltos*, meaning "secure."[3] The Babylonians used it to build roads, as did the Romans, who also used it to seal their baths and aqueducts.[4] It has a long and illustrious history.

With the advent of the automobile industry and the consequent expansion of paved roads, the market for asphalt grew exponentially. Most fortuitously, asphalt is also a by-product of petroleum refining, which is necessary to provide the energy that is still used to power vehicles and industries.

The asphalt pavement industry is a significant sector of the United States infrastructure and makes up a considerable portion of the U.S. economy. It employs well over 750,000 workers in direct and related industries, including:[5]

- 343,120 people in the construction of highway, streets, runways, roads, and bridges
- 59,860 operating heavy construction equipment
- 243,840 people in civil, environmental, and geotechnical engineering
- 111,470 in the refining sector

Annual infrastructure investment by federal, state, and local governments in the United States was estimated at about 1.5 percent of GDP in 2016.[6] A significant part of that investment is the approximately 450 million tons of hot-mix asphalt (HMA) that is produced and placed each year. The total expenditure for asphalt pavement surfaces is in excess of $25 billion annually.[7] In an even broader look at highways and roads throughout the nation, they move 72 percent or nearly $17 trillion of the country's goods.[8]

Finally, an interesting and important fact is that asphalt pavement is the number-one recycled product in America. By a lot. The industry has been leading the charge on recycling for decades, and it's proud of that fact. The uniqueness and flexibility of asphalt pavements also allow for other materials, in practical amounts, to be reused and recycled by incorporating tire rubber, asphalt shingles, and even glass into the mixtures.

The Asphalt Pavement Ecosystem

The asphalt pavement industry supply chain is vast, and it is made up of three primary material sectors: the asphalt binder (bitumen), additive suppliers and manufacturers (chemicals), and aggregates (stone, sand, and gravel):

1. *The asphalt binder.* The binder in asphalt pavement is the asphalt itself in liquid form, which makes up about 5 percent of the pavement mix. This sector utilizes the byproduct (asphalt) of crude oil refining and also includes natural asphalt.

2. *Additive suppliers/manufacturing.* This sector represents the additives that are manufactured by the suppliers. They include chemicals and other bio-based products, which include soy oil derivatives, lignin, and biochar. These are used to modify the binders that are critical to some mixtures, their quality, and performance.

3. *The aggregates.* This is the asphalt pavement industry ecosystem's central component; it is the aggregates that feed into the production of mix and construction. The primary aggregates (or materials) used in asphalt pavement are stone, sand, and gravel. This sector includes mining and dredging, after which the aggregates are processed: crushed, washed, sized, and so forth. Each of the three sectors feeds into other important layers of the industry's supply chain including transportation (water, rail, and truck) and manufacturing

(testing, paving, fleet vehicles, terminals, storage, safety equipment, construction equipment, and plants). From there, asphalt pavement industry mixture production and construction commences, and asphalt is applied in an array of end uses including highways, streets, roads, bridge deck surfaces, runways, and commercial and private applications such as racetracks parking lots, driveways, agriculture facilities, shipping yards, recreation (trails, sports courts), and environmental liners for water reservoirs, landfills, and so forth.

There is another consideration that is critical to the asphalt pavement industry, though not technically part of the supply chain. The majority of paved streets, roads, boulevards, and highways in America are owned by local, state, and federal governments, which fund the bulk of the industry's construction projects. Thus, governments choose infrastructure priorities and the construction and maintenance projects for our nation's roadway infrastructure, and government officials also set the standards and tests for the product. See Figure 6.1.

National Asphalt Pavement Association (NAPA)

The National Asphalt Pavement Association (NAPA) is the only national association representing the interests of asphalt mixture producers and represents the asphalt pavement industry in several important senses of the word.

First, it represents the industry in the sense that it is officially appointed to speak (and, when necessary, act) on behalf of its 1,200 members to the government and other interested parties, including Congress, federal regulators and other federal agencies, state departments of transportation (DOTs), labor unions, and various business

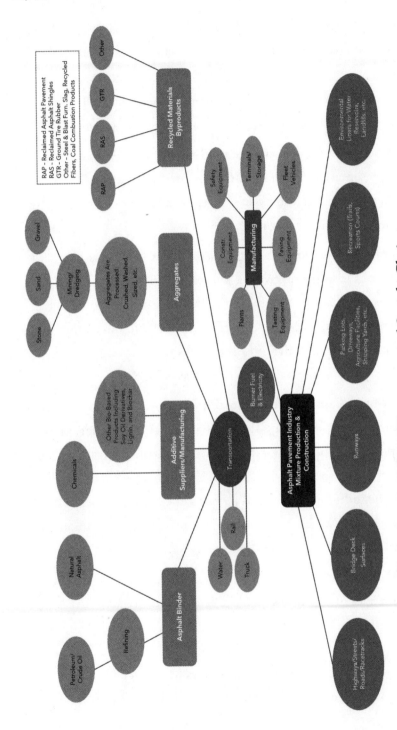

Figure 6.1 The Asphalt Pavement Industry Ecosystem and Supply Chain
Source: Illustration artwork prepared by Erin Wagner, Edge Research.

and trade associations. For example, NAPA extends the industry's strategic partnership reach through its leadership roles in transportation and infrastructure coalitions such as the Transportation Construction Coalition, the U.S. Chamber of Commerce Americans for Transportation Mobility Coalition, and the Highway Materials Group.

Second, NAPA represents the industry in the sense that it is a broad representation of the industry not only geographically across the United States, but also by size, revenue, and focus (binders, aggregates, and manufacturing).

Third, NAPA represents the industry in the sense that it is a reflection of the impressive values and capabilities of the industry. The industry values its workforce and their safety and protection, advancement of knowledge, and engineering of and innovation for asphalt pavements, and the industry knows that a robust, well-funded pavement system is the backbone of our economy.

Jim Mitchell, president of Superior Paving Corporation and first vice chairman of NAPA, says that "What NAPA does, what it has always done, is to be collaborative and forward-thinking and practical in everything they do." He goes on to say that "We have the lion's share of the industry represented by our association . . . most importantly, by talent. We have some amazing, amazing people among our membership."

NAPA represents the industry so well because it has so many representatives of the industry in the association. In fact, NAPA represents well over 70 percent of the asphalt mixtures produced in the United States and its territories. "Whenever it's time to tackle a new challenge or even a new opportunity," says Mr. Mitchell, "we don't have to make many calls to get the right people at the table."

Leadership

When you think about industry leadership and what it means in the context of asphalt pavement, it is defined by strategic collaboration and what industry executives do together. In a business led primarily by skilled executives, they are data driven, results focused, and use science and research to support their bias for action. These are the defining attributes of industry leaders, and they wanted their next trade association leader to mirror these with industry background and technical knowledge. In fact, in the 66 years that NAPA has been in existence, there have been three presidents (before that, the member volunteers handled all association business),[9] and they have all come from the roads industry with an extensive technical background and have demonstrated continuity, stability, and the value of expertise in pavement design and construction.

The first person to hold the title of president, John Gray, was formerly a director of public works for a city in Maryland championing innovations in asphalt pavement maintenance. The second president, Mike Acott, also had a technical background and joined NAPA after working in the asphalt industry in South Africa. He was an engineer (a physics major and civil engineer) and came to NAPA as head of engineering and then moved into the president role. The current president and CEO is Audrey Copeland, appointed in 2019, a former highway engineer and researcher for the Federal Highway Administration (FHWA) and the head of NAPA's engineering team for seven years, similar to Mike Acott. Copeland has over 20 years of experience in asphalt mixtures and pavements including a Doctorate in Civil Engineering, as well as being a licensed professional engineer.

As the CEO, Copeland also brought valuable and natural (for her) skills to the table. At her core, she is a tremendous collaborator and continually connects with industry audiences to define and deliver solutions. Humility is critical from an industry perspective, especially when it comes to leadership. Every executive leads and learns: it is an integral part of their industry DNA, and the industry's acknowledgment of her skills and background is evident.

Her industry knowledge and continual focus on data and outcomes is making a difference. Jim Mitchell had this to say: "She's abundantly qualified to do her job. She's smart. She's well-educated in the fields that she needs to be. She has a passion for what we're doing." Describing her leadership style, he uses an illustration of how a boat captain steers a ship: "She's back there holding the tiller, setting the course and the direction, and she's bringing the right people on board to power the boat. But she's the one steering it . . . And she leads from humility, which is also very important."

Business Acumen

Beyond technical knowledge of the industry and credentials, NAPA members know that the president and CEO must also be able to think like them, business owners and executives, and anticipate and manage short- and long-term risks and opportunities. When I asked Kurt Bechthold, chairman and CEO of the Walbec Group Co., to talk about business acumen, his response was this:

> That's what I'm talking about when I talk about *it*. I'm talking about somebody who just gets it. And business acumen is kind of central to that. There are some people who are very good

technically and who can see incremental change. There are very few people that I know that can really see a big picture, and think ahead five steps, and understand how finance interplays with safety, and that interplays with personnel, and that interplays with marketing. To be able to keep all those balls in the air and understand the interaction between all of them, you might sum it up as business acumen. But I just look at it as *it*.

Mr. Bechthold was on the search committee that selected Copeland from a pool of six finalists to take over in 2019. Before that, Mike Acott had served as NAPA's president for 30 years, steering the industry through growth and success in navigating serious threats as well as opportunities. They were big shoes to fill. From Mr. Bechthold's perspective, the new leader had to be a big thinker, strategic rather than tactical; a capable manager, obviously, because they would be managing people, but mostly a big thinker. The ability to think strategically, to rethink the business model going forward, to think about wholesale change rather than incremental change: those items on his checklist were nonnegotiable. He sees a sea change coming, and he is quite certain they are going to need someone who has what he describes simply as *it*.

Jim Mitchell believes the biggest element of business acumen is managing risk. Mr. Mitchell explained his thinking along these lines:

> Some would say business acumen means you've got to charge more than you spend. That's true. Others say it's the ability to get the right people on your team. That's also true. You do need the right people on your team. Others say it's about having the right perspective and the right insights into your business, the ability to look forward the right amount of distance. If you're driving a car

and you only look five feet in front of you, it's not going to go well. Now there are times that you need to be paying a lot of attention to what's five feet in front of you, but you also need to be looking a mile ahead.

In sum, it is all about how you manage risk. And just like NAPA members handle risk within their companies and projects every day, NAPA staff, under the leadership of the NAPA president and CEO, must manage the risks and opportunities for an entire industry. There is reassurance in knowing someone is looking out for the industry. Jim concluded his thoughts on the subject this way:

> I would dare say if the whole country understood what managing risk even means, we'd have a greater understanding of what makes our economy work. I have to do that every day with our company. And Audrey has to do that every day at NAPA. And there are sunny days and there are days where the storms are brewing. And you have to be able to look at the situation, both near and far off, and assess the risk and how best to navigate it. And that's what we do as business owners every day, and NAPA and Audrey do that very well. And then everything trickles down from there.

NAPA and the Asphalt Pavement Industry: Anatomy of a Strategic Partnership

The industry embraces NAPA, and they view the trade association as the industry and an exceedingly important partner on many fronts. The industry insists on a high-quality standard in all of its projects, it emphasizes the value it delivers to its customers, and together they are determined to deliver enhanced mobility and a thriving and sustainable transportation network throughout the United States. The trade association reflects these strong principles, and it serves as a dynamic gathering place to advance the industry's outcomes. From its beginnings through today, NAPA is the industry's principle go-to-market vehicle. From networking to advocacy and engineering, the trade association is the industry's platform to help shape the external environment, increase asphalt's relevance, and optimize its utilization throughout the country.

The industry trade association is especially a valuable resource for small, medium, and large asphalt pavement enterprises. In many cases, its members do not have the capabilities to accomplish the important tasks necessary to be effective in the marketplace. When it comes to making a case to elected officials and regulators, a large group of the members do not have lobbyists on staff, or an engineering and research team, or, in some cases, an environmental, health, and safety officer. NAPA provides that additional expertise for companies.

Copeland said:

Our members very much value having subject matter experts on staff as an association. In that sense, they view us as their staff and their partners in the D.C. area or in these certain subjects that they don't have the bandwidth to hire a dedicated person, whether it's engineering, whether it's environmental health and safety, whether it's marketing of the industry, they really look to us to have that expertise. I think that in some cases makes us unique from other associations.

Shared Values

The principal values that NAPA and the larger asphalt pavement industry share are:

- Trust
- Expertise
- Sustainability (doing the right thing)
- Community focus

Trust

The asphalt pavement industry continually seeks and it proactively employs a transparent approach to everything it does. Serving as the industry, NAPA mirrors the greater asphalt community and seeks truth; it collaborates on and shares data to reach sound conclusions. It reaches truth through research and knowledge and partnering with others. From an engineering perspective, it makes perfect sense; NAPA wants to understand the facts and learn more about threats and where the industry stands so the association can appropriately address them. This is how it builds trust among its members, among their customers, among the workforce, and among regulators, and it works.

Expertise

As noted, NAPA's leadership people all had technical and engineering expertise, and the majority of NAPA's executive staff are subject-matter experts in their respective fields. What is most striking is how small- and medium-sized companies' technical expertise is utilized. These firms have served the industry by informing government agencies such as FHWA (Federal Highway Administration), EPA (Environmental Protection Agency), OSHA (Occupational Safety and Health Administration), NIOSH (National Institute for Occupational Safety and Health), and State DOTS (Department of Transportation), etc., and they lead important research and initiatives that resulted in changes in the way asphalt pavements are specified, tested, and evaluated for improved quality and performance.

NAPA and the industry respect and value science, research, and engineering, and it takes the time to engage, build partnerships, and design solutions on multiple fronts. A primary example is the industry's endowment of the National Center for Asphalt Technology (NCAT) at Auburn University. NCAT was seeded by the industry through NAPA and has been so successful that it is now over 90 percent funded by the Federal Highway Administration (FHWA) and State Departments of Transportation (DOTs). NCAT's impressive level of expertise has built a strong foundation of credibility and been influential with helping define state DOTs' specifications, especially in the southeastern part of the country. NCAT also provides an experiment environment, including a test track and loading from multiple fully loaded 18-wheeler trucks, for governments and companies to try innovations in asphalt pavement design and construction.

An April 2021 report and case study that highlights the capabilities of asphalt pavements to improve transportation infrastructure resilience[10] is an example of this work. The report, developed by Benjamin Bowers, PhD, PE, of Auburn University and Fan Gu, PhD, PE, supplies important background and research that reveals the asphalt industry's resilience strategies. Published by NAPA, the conclusive report documents an innovative use of existing technologies and practices that can enhance the resilience of asphalt pavements.

Bowers and Gu note the ability of these as well as future tools to create "the more resilient pavement network of the future." In underscoring their point, they indicate that roadway resilience isn't limited to a structure itself, but it does include entire transportation systems as well as the overall communities they serve.

When you look at this level of expertise there is a straight line to how over time the industry, through NAPA, has invested in and built out a strong foundation. There are many examples of how this expertise helps the industry. For instance, in the latter portion of the twentieth century, FHWA led the asphalt pavement mixture design and tested it through the Strategic Highway Research Program (SHRP), a multimillion-dollar effort to improve the design of pavements. Now it is industry and academia, along with FHWA, leading the way through a concept called Balanced Mix Design, focused on pavement performance rather than recipe specifications. This industry is fueled by science and data; it's an invaluable resource that demonstrates a growing brand reputation steeped in expertise.

Sustainability (Doing the Right Thing)

The asphalt industry understands well how sustainable practices contributing to a clean environment can result in cost savings and good business practices, and it routinely takes the necessary steps to make that happen. Let us take an even closer look at the asphalt industry ecosystem and supply chain to learn more details about its commitment to cost savings and sustainability. You will note the discussion of recycled materials byproducts, and we already noted how much of a leader this industry is in recycling. The fact is that companies in this industry utilize a lot of recycled products in the materials they use to lay down asphalt pavement. The noteworthy list of recycled products includes reclaimed asphalt pavement (RAP), reclaimed asphalt shingles (RAS), ground tire rubber (GTR), air cooled blast furnace slag, recycled fibers, and coal combustion products. Each of these products plays a role in helping the industry continually implement its sustainability promise.

The industry proudly reflects its ongoing commitments: "demonstrating our environmental stewardship practices in a visible and tangible way certainly provides a culture that is attractive to the younger—and older—generation of workers," says Denise Hallett Manager of Community and Government Outreach, Vulcan Materials Co., Mideast Division. "When the space they work in looks good and they see the company investing in programs that enhance the environment, it's a win for both of us."[11]

It doesn't stop there, either. "An important part of sustainability for asphalt plants is how the facility fits into and works with the natural environment around it. By establishing wildlife habitats at asphalt plants, it shows a company's commitment to supporting and enhancing the environments in which we work and sends a powerful message to our neighbors," adds Ron Sines, PE, Vice President Performance—Asphalt at CRH Americas Materials, Inc.[12]

NAPA very much reflects the industry's values and commitments when it comes to sustainability. The trade association is quite innovative in its own right and developed ready-to-use resources to help its members and the industry implement sustainability practices on an ongoing basis. The impressive list of resources includes a green-house gas calculator, an environmental product declaration tool to measure the environmental impact of asphalt mixes, and an energy star partnership (between NAPA and the U.S. Environmental Protection Agency [EPA]), which is a pilot program to help in the reduction of energy consumption and related costs at mixture production facilities.[13]

Jim Mitchell reminded me that the sustainability and carbon conversation is not new. "It's in a different gear right now," he agreed, "but we're actually having those conversations now, where we're engaging with federal authorities and industry partners to see what we can do." He points out that the industry has been leading the way for years, and it's important that the message gets out. "We've already done so much awesome work. We've been able to take our mix temperatures and reduce them by 15% to 20%. We've done all this work to reduce the amount of energy we use in our process and to improve sustainability by including recycle as part of our finished product. And we've been doing that for years, long before it was cool; longer than it's been a lead story on the news."

Community Focus

Jay Winford is the president of Prairie Contractors in southern Louisiana. He is also the current chairman of NAPA. He has a keen sense of both the importance and the desirability of community. It is a staple in his own life and experience, and it is deeply embedded in his psyche. You might say he lives and breathes a sense of caring and community. In 2020, Louisiana endured several hurricanes that directly impacted Jay's company's operations, and here is one of his thoughts on the subject:

> There are so many stories written after these hurricanes and these wildfires. The industry takes care of each other. After the last two hurricanes that hit us, I had calls from North Carolina and Minnesota. "What do you need?" my fellow NAPA members asked me. "We'll send a pick-up down there. We'll go to Lowe's." . . . We take care of each other. And I'm very proud of that. And I think . . . the NAPA staff recognizes that, too.

Looking back in history, the majority of asphalt pavement companies doing business in the United States have been local or regional, family-owned companies —especially because the product must be produced close to where it is used or paved. Many companies today are still family-owned, some third and fourth generation, and they are proud of it. A Google search for "family-owned asphalt pavement companies" returns thousands of results. The majority of the first several hundred results are in fact asphalt paving companies that describe themselves as "family-owned and operated." Other popular descriptions include such words and phrases as "local," "regional," "second-, third-, or fourth-generation," and "full service."

In the latter half of the twentieth century, industry companies realized the benefits of vertical integration in order to own and control the raw materials and to be able to compete for pavement construction projects. Thus, there was growth in international and national companies acquiring asphalt plants as well as quarries and asphalt terminals. Further, asphalt mixture companies have expanded regionally to diversify their business. The industry is now a mixture of international, national, regional, and local companies with 3,000 to 4,000 plants across the United States at a given time. But the heart and soul of the industry and its ethos is still grounded in a deep sense of community.

Jay Winford spoke further of his own experience relating to community:

> We want to create a safe haven, whether it's in NAPA when we're together or a subset where a group of us want to dive deeper and say: I want to be a good manager. I want to be a good coworker. I want to be a good dad. And I want to create an environment for my people that they really want to get up in the morning and come to work and want to be here.
>
> And they're working in a good culture. When we have hurricanes and the roof of their house gets damaged, we jump in there and help them. It's a family.

The asphalt pavement industry was built by smart, solid, thoughtful, reliable Americans. And the men and women who built it passed along those attributes to their children and grandchildren. This industry, though it has grown and evolved, is still infused with some traditional family characteristics. It is an industry that values the family, that cares about its people, and that seeks the good of the community. From their vantage point, gatherings that bring the industry together to network and learn, the annual convention, and midyear meetings at NAPA are all viewed as essential and relevant to keeping the community networked with one another.

Shared Outcomes: Industry and NAPA Partnerships

As we have discussed, shared outcomes is another attribute that matters if a strategic partnership is to be successful. Let us see how that is playing out in the asphalt pavement industry's partnership with NAPA.

Environmental Product Declarations (EPDs) and Reducing Environmental Impact

Copeland speaks of an opportunity that NAPA identified over five years ago, a new challenge that is on the near horizon, which seems to be more relevant now as the conversation on climate change intensifies. "What we're seeing now across products, across all industries, is what's called environmental product declarations (EPDs). What it boils down to is it's essentially a nutrition label for a product that tells you what the environmental impact is." NAPA identified early on that road owners and customers would eventually want to know the environmental impacts of materials and road construction. In fact, during President Obama's administration, some of the trade association's members were already starting to get requests for EPDs.
The NAPA team invested much time and resources developing a robust EPD program for the industry based on international guidelines. Now, as climate change has become more urgent and localities are requiring EPDs, NAPA members have a readily available, scientifically sound, approved tool to generate the EPDs.

Kurt Bechthold said, "If I look at NAPA in terms of their lanes of expertise—including environmental—I appreciate that they're helping develop EPDs, which are going to be a standard going forward, I believe. And rather than having everybody invent it on their own, to have one person be an expert on it is very helpful."

In short, it's very much about transparency. Copeland elaborates:

Just like you see a nutrition label on your box of cookies or your box of cereal, that tells you calories and sugar and protein and all that, the EPD provides information on the environmental and/or climate impact of materials, chemicals, or manufacturing processes, and so forth.

We saw this coming. And there's no way any company could have just developed this on their own, or even in collaboration with a few other companies. This was a huge undertaking because you have to develop rules and requirements around the product that are verified by an independent, third-party panel, you have extensive data collection for life-cycle inventory and analysis, and development of assessments and software, in order to produce the EPD. It's actually a multi-step process that's laid out and defined by ISO (International Organization for Standardization), and it has to be recertified every five years or so.

NAPA led the way. They chose to proactively study, measure, and quantify the environmental and climate impact of the materials and processes used across the asphalt pavement industry. And now it is in place. Member companies can simply fill in the relevant information from their own companies, and the software template will make all of the necessary calculations to provide a finished and accurate EPD. NAPA felt it had to do it. Not only was the writing on the wall, but it was the right thing to do. NAPA's members rely on them. And NAPA was pretty much the only one that could have done it.

Of course, because it was ahead of its time, it was not a simple, clear-cut decision. It required some finesse. Copeland elaborates:

> Now the challenge is we couldn't look at it necessarily in the beginning as a revenue source for the association because EPDs weren't required or largely being requested yet. So, there's nothing that's causing our members to have to take it up, or to have to start producing EPDs. But we knew that eventually it was going to come. Either road owners were going to start requesting it or it could potentially be required by law. And that's where we're at now. We're starting to see legislation introduced in localities and states that would require EPDs for construction materials.

Warm Mix Asphalt

Warm mix asphalt (WMA) was developed to lower the heat, and thus energy, to produce asphalt mixtures. Warm mix asphalt allows the industry to produce mixtures at a lower temperature, thereby saving on fuel costs as well as emissions. Once early adopters began implementing the new process, however, serendipity stepped in. Several unexpected benefits were quickly revealed.

The first added benefit was constructability. WMA allows crews to construct the pavement more quickly and easily. The second added benefit was worker comfort in working with mixtures with a lower temperature.

Copeland had more to say on the subject:

> When you're building a pavement with asphalt, even though we can quickly reopen to traffic (in fact, we are the quickest pavement

to be reopen[ed] to traffic), after you put the asphalt down, you still have to compact it, or roll it, because you're trying to reach a certain density for quality. And what we found is that with warm mix asphalt you could possibly take one of the roller passes off; you could lower the number of passes. Or you could even take one of the rollers off, thereby saving money and saving time.

Fuel savings did materialize for the industry by lowering mix temperatures. And there were substantial local savings related to the time for construction. But in terms of savings for our country, they were significant. In 2004, the industry led the first WMA pilot projects in the United States, which soon prompted FHWA to explore the technology and support research into WMA. FHWA and NAPA established a joint technical working group for WMA,[14] which resulted in over $10 million worth of research funding that proved out the technologies—ensuring quality and pavement performance.

In 2010, the FHWA adopted warm mix asphalt technology as part of its Every Day Counts[15] initiative to quickly roll out market ready technologies to state DOTs and local highway agencies. In 2014, U.S. Secretary of Transportation Anthony Foxx commented that "the use of WMA is expected to save $3.6 billion in energy costs alone by 2020."[16] And now, WMA technologies make up almost 40 percent of the asphalt pavement market and the industry is turning its focus to realize the full potential of WMA by further reducing production temperatures.

NAPA's Strategic Partnerships on Behalf of the Industry

According to Copeland, NAPA's most important strategic relationships (after the industry itself) are with the agencies that regulate or specify conditions in terms of road projects and plants. They amplify each other's shared values and shared outcomes, especially relating to workers, worker safety, the environment, and meeting quality and performance specifications.

Trust is also important. Copeland believes that the common thread that runs through all of NAPA's activities and engagements and endeavors is partnerships, relationships, and alliances. Rather than combatting every regulatory issue that comes up, NAPA works closely with the regulatory agencies and with the labor unions. There are times when they disagree, "but when we all come to the table and at least talk about it, that's huge, and solutions are often found and quickly implemented by the industry."

It works along these lines: If some new regulation is coming out that could challenge the industry, before jumping to conclusions and making rash decisions, they choose to understand the issue. They choose to assess objectively how it might impact the industry. In most cases, they end up not needing to fight it. Instead, they decide to work with the regulatory agency, to partner with them. Even though they may be coming at the problem from two different viewpoints, by trusting that each wants the best for both the industry and the people they both serve, they often reach agreement on the common outcome they both want.

The regulatory agencies with which they have had working relationships and strategic alliances are: the Occupational Safety and Health Administration (OSHA), the National Institute for Occupational Safety and Health (NIOSH), and the Environmental Protection Agency (EPA).

NAPA's Strategic Partnerships to Improve Worker Health and Safety

NAPA's leadership in helping industry find ways to improve worker health and safety has been well-documented over the last three decades. NAPA's approach, to voluntarily partner with relevant stakeholders across government, academia, labor, and industry, has resulted in successful technological advances in an industry historically slow to adopt change.

Engineering Controls on Asphalt Paving Machines

During the 1990s, OSHA began to focus agency efforts on lowering applicable occupational exposure criteria across all industries. Not waiting for regulation to dictate action and recognizing worker safety and comfort always has potential for improvement, NAPA initiated and led a multistakeholder approach to effectively control paving emissions. This effort, the first in a series of national efforts and partnerships between NAPA, industry, labor, and government agencies, resulted in the voluntary implementation of new engineering controls for paving equipment.[17]

Jay Winford describes NAPA's response to this idea that there may be ways to improve worker safety and comfort:

> NAPA got all of the paving equipment manufacturers together, and they said, "It will be pretty easy for us to take some fans and extend some exhaust, and whether there's a problem or not, let's get all that way above our people." So, you know what? The industry themselves—without government regulations—developed what we called engineering controls. It's now on every paver that's manufactured. We solved the problem.

The really interesting and telling thing about that is the fact that the industry took it upon themselves to solve any potential problem, from within. From their perspective, protecting its workers remains at the top of the industry's priority list.

Silica/Asphalt Milling Machine Partnership

One serious health and safety challenge the industry faced—and conquered through a brilliantly conceived and executed strategic partnership that continues to this day—was around silica dust control. Copeland told me the story for historical reference:

> Contractors mill up old pavements which contain aggregate. There was a possibility that as we're milling up these old pavements, silica dust is introduced into the air. In the mid-2010s, OSHA announced the agency was contemplating lowering its acceptable worker exposure threshold for silica dust. And we knew silica had been found to be a respiratory irritant and also could lead to illness. Rather than refute or oppose the agency, NAPA relied on its history of voluntary stakeholder participation to solve problems, and again formed a partnership with the labor unions and with the government agencies to explore how the industry could meet any upcoming agency silica dust standard using equipment controls rather than making our workers don respiratory masks or suits.

In 2003, NAPA formed the Silica/Asphalt Milling Machine Partnership to study milling machine dust controls. The partnership included many of their own members (mostly equipment manufacturers and paving contractors), the International Union of Operating Engineers, the Laborers International Union of North America, the Association of Equipment Manufacturers, OSHA, and the Center for Disease Control's (CDC's) NIOSH. Coordinated by NAPA, the partnership included all U.S. and foreign manufacturers of heavy construction equipment that sell pavement-milling machines to the U.S. market.[18]

Copeland continued:

This voluntary partnership ended up being very successful. In fact, OSHA eventually issued its silica dust rule based on industry-developed engineering controls, validated by CDC/NIOSH. This type of industry-government-labor partnership has been formally recognized as a gold standard for helping spur voluntary technology advancements to improve worker health and safety. It resulted in us being formally recognized by NIOSH, and I think it was one of the first official recognitions of an association. And even though it was a group effort, the credit is given to NAPA for coordinating that entire process.

Jay Winford told me the silica story from his perspective:

God made our environment. It's either normal and perfect, or it's dry, or it's wet. And when it's dry, there's dust. And we don't want people breathing in dust, particularly since it's associated with silica. We've done a lot of studies on our own through NAPA that I can't do on my own.

Here's how Jim Mitchell remembers it:

Silica continues to be a topic of conversation. Our industry went out to the right people that might regulate these types of things as well as those with the capacity to study them. And we got together and said, "Okay, let's walk through our process and let's understand what our challenges are." And you can imagine on the first day of that we didn't know all that we needed to know. Therefore, while we might feel like we were going to come out of that in a good spot, we didn't know.

Our company went out and hired a [research] company ourselves. And we did studies on every position in our company and in our organization before even NAPA got to it. And my point is we as a company, and many other companies, are proactive enough about safety and health, that we went out and did those things right away. And our results came back, and we shared them with NAPA along with other members.

They continued to do their testing and it all has concluded that we don't have a challenge except in very isolated situations where we, as a company, make sure those equipment operators are now in enclosed cabs with proper ventilation and filters.

We've been able to eliminate all of those concerns in our operation through adapting our equipment. And the equipment manufactures partnered with us, too. So, it wasn't a matter of having to spend five years figuring out the answer. We had the solution almost as soon as we had the answer.

NAPA's Strategic Partnerships to Advance Pavement Technologies

While NAPA members are busy producing infrastructure materials and building pavements, they rely on NAPA to advocate for resources to improve materials and pavements for highways and other critical applications and be their voice in partnering with the U.S. DOT and, more specifically, federal agencies within the U.S. DOT, such as FHWA and the Federal Aviation Administration (FAA).

NAPA has an especially strong strategic partnership with FHWA. Although not a regulatory agency, FHWA "are stewards," says Copeland, "of the federal money for highways and roads. They make sure that the federal highway funding money is spent properly. And so, they set policies and issue guidance that our members' customers follow. It's imperative we have a very good relationship with FHWA, and I think they understand the importance of industry input."

Taking Time to Develop the FHWA Relationship

Audrey Copeland planned to be a college professor, which is the reason she gives for having pursued (and achieved) advanced degrees, including a PhD in civil engineering. She was grateful to be offered a fellowship from the federal government to do her research as part of her PhD. That fellowship was with FHWA.

"And that's when," Copeland recalls, "I really started to learn the value of these relationships. And it also helped that I was young and new to DC, and I didn't know anyone. So it was really important that while I'm developing these work relationships, they also served as kind of an extension of friends and family."

Through the process of getting to know different people, opportunities opened up for her. After finishing her studies, Copeland was hired on at FHWA. When the FHWA was considering adopting warm mix asphalt as one of their key innovations, for example, they tapped Copeland to present that innovative technology to FHWA's leadership.

FHWA recognized the value of bringing industry to the table because at that time the industry was leading on WMA through NAPA. And that is how Copeland began interacting with NAPA. She had mentors in FHWA who truly saw the value of industry/government partnerships and provided opportunities for Copeland to work with NAPA and get to know NAPA as an association.

Copeland was both intrigued and impressed by the association and joined NAPA in 2012 as the vice president of engineering, research, and technology. Through her relationships, she worked diligently to deliver advancement opportunities for the industry at large in her new role.

An Unconventional Strategic Partnership to Secure Funding for Advancing Pavement Technologies

Much federal government funding toward highways had been spent on research and development of technology and, around 2012, the industry felt it was now time to implement those technologies to further improve pavement performance.

NAPA's government affairs department, meanwhile, had been working in collaboration with the American Concrete Pavement Association (ACPA) on securing funding dedicated to implementing pavement technology. Remarkable is the fact that ACPA represents the concrete paving industry, the primary competitor for asphalt pavements.

Copeland supplied the NAPA government affairs team with technical information that, in partnership with ACPA, convinced Congress to establish a program, funded at $12 million annually, for accelerated implementation and deployment of pavement technologies (known as the AID-PT program)[19]—essentially taking proven research to market to improve our nation's highways. Copeland tells it like this:

> What I would highlight (since we talked so much about the government partnerships, especially FHWA), is what I mentioned with that $12 million we secured through Congress. That was actually

a partnership with the American Concrete Pavement Association, and I don't think we would have been able to secure that $12 million without us going in together on that. And so, even though we compete, we know when to work together, we know when it's important to both of our industries. That time, our partnership resulted in technology deployment money in the millions for advancing each industry.

Beyond Advocacy: Strategic Partnering for Shared Outcomes

Since NAPA values technical expertise and has subject matter experts on staff, when it came time to execute on the FHWA pavement technology program, NAPA leadership gave Copeland the blessing to compete for an FHWA cooperative agreement with funding of $2.5 million over five years to advance asphalt pavement technologies. The cooperative agreement is a partnership between FHWA and the agreement awardee, and the agreement specifies financial commitments not only from the government but also from the agreement awardee, meaning industry, though NAPA would also be invested in this agreement and the outcomes. NAPA worked very hard preparing extensive technical and cost proposals and they partnered with the National Center for Asphalt Technology (NCAT), other universities, and consultants to bring the requisite expertise to the table. It was the first time in NAPA's history that the trade association was awarded a government cooperative agreement. Both FHWA and NAPA valued a mutual trust in each other to advance pavement technology and the importance of applying technical expertise to improve technology and the products they use. Copeland drove home the importance of this particular shared value:

What that meant to the industry is that we were partners with FHWA in leading the way in putting out guidance, and the knowledge to deploy these technologies such as warm mix asphalt, recycled pavements, and thin asphalt overlays. These were technologies that the industry believed in, that they knew would make a difference not only to our highways, but also to their bottom line. And because we have the technical expertise and have the relationship with the government and State DOTs through our State Asphalt Pavement Associations, NAPA was well-positioned to be able to successfully carry that out.

The more specific outcomes of the FHWA-industry partnership are detailed in annual reports for the AID-PT program.[20]

NAPA and ACPA have joined forces again over the past few years to secure dedicated research funding for airfield pavements. Both industries' members realized the need to update and advance specifications and technologies for airfield pavements. And once again they have been successful, primarily through NAPA's relationships and leadership in government affairs. In fact, in a mildly uncanny replay of the FHWA story, NAPA's current lead engineer developed outstanding relationships within the FAA in the area of technical expertise and knowledge sharing. Again, with NAPA staff being technical experts in asphalt technology, the FAA asked NAPA to help manage the program rather than a research institute or university. NAPA worked with the FAA to form a joint oversight group, and this setup, with NAPA coordinating, provides opportunities for the leading institutions and researchers to compete for research project funding without having to deal with the program administration. Copeland extols the value of this award:

So not only does that help NAPA pay for our staff time and bring us some non-dues revenue, the anticipated outcome is that the research will result in possible changes to specifications. This will benefit our members in terms of what FAA requires of airfield pavements, whether it's specification changes that can save costs, or advancing research that is ready to be implemented.

Current and Future Outcomes

Copeland recognizes that there is still work to be done to solidify strategic alliances, especially with the state DOTs, through NAPA's relationship with the FHWA:

> We've had another huge initiative for the past few years that I was leading when I was in the engineering role. Right now, our customers (the state DOTs), usually make us follow a "recipe" to either produce asphalt or to build roads. They're setting certain parameters. We would like to get to the point where we can say, "You know what, let us focus on the outcome. You just tell us what kind of road you want, or what kind of mix you want, and the performance you want, and let us focus on the outcome, and let us focus on which materials we use. Let us focus on performance rather than on a recipe."

> That has really taken hold and it's advancing very quickly through the industry, thanks to NAPA's leadership. And that's another reason that we're going to have to keep these strategic partnerships going. Success depends on those relationships because the state DOTs and FHWA are the ones that are going to be setting what tests you might have to do to make sure the performance is there.

Ultimately, whether it's FHWA or the FAA, NAPA is aligned with government partners in outcomes. NAPA and the asphalt pavement industry quite fervently share that mutual desire to continually improve the nation's roadways and airfields as part of our transportation network. Well-performing, high-functioning pavements are, quite simply, the pride of the industry.

The Future of the Asphalt Pavement Industry

As the industry looks to the future, there are a number of things on the horizon. Most important is a sustainable highway funding source since the current model currently relies on the gas tax. There is also the need to advance technology in construction to improve production times, safety, and value.

Beyond these challenges are those for identifying opportunities in using roads beyond surface transportation—for example, for carbon capture, energy harnessing, or energy generation. These are all trends and indications of potential change that will need to be watched very closely indeed. With regard to how things will actually play out, it is anybody's guess. There are some compelling arguments, as you will see later, for any number of possible futures for the asphalt pavement industry. Each interpretation is valid, but only one is correct. And we probably won't know which one until the future is upon us.

But as Copeland looks beyond the horizon, she sees another challenge. Careful observers know that the asphalt pavement industry depends almost exclusively for its binder on asphalt as a by-product of petroleum refining. As noted earlier, asphalt is naturally occurring, but not in the quantities necessary to sustain the industry economically. As essentially a waste product from the oil industry, asphalt plays an unusually useful role. But that may change with a shift in energy sources to power vehicles. Here are some prognostications from NAPA's leadership.

Kurt Bechthold:

I think as we move toward electrification for vehicles, there's going to be a shift in our business model across the country. I think NAPA can play a leading role in that. We know that electrification is going to happen to vehicles going forward. We know that our funding sources traditionally have been centered on gas tax. Well, the two of those don't play well towards the future.

Asphalt is a by-product. And if they don't make gasoline and diesel, they won't make asphalt. Or if they do, it will be very expensive, and we'll be priced out of the market. Historically asphalt is the bottom of the oil barrel. It's an oil-based product. If the country's going to use less oil, that's going to impact our ability to survive. What new products need to be developed so that we can continue to make asphalt? Because if they're not refining oil, they're not making asphalt. If they're not making asphalt, there is no asphalt industry. And if there is no asphalt industry, NAPA—as it is now—doesn't exist.

We're on the precipice of wholesale change. There will be need for new and different binders, there will be need for new funding sources. If you go down the path of new binders, there will be need for new specifications. It'll have to be marketed differently. There may or may not be environmental consequences of all that. It really truly is a once-in-a-lifetime wholesale change that we're looking at in the next 15 years.

To go back to my business school days, this is truly a buggy whip moment. And I think that there are very few people in our industry right now that really have thought it through well enough to understand what's coming down the railroad tracks at us. But there is a bright light at the end of the tunnel, and I think it's a train coming. And I think Audrey, because of her technical knowledge and her ability to think big, I think she's very well positioned to help us get through that.

Jim Mitchell:

I just spent the weekend out west where there's not many people. And you've got to drive a long way to get from one town to the next. And I remember I was actually going for a walk and I went underneath this power line. It wasn't a very big power line, but it stretched a long way. And I thought that thing is going to have to be a lot bigger if we're all driving electric cars. And so to me, people's perspective on the horizon for this awesome future of electric transportation is much further out than people think it is.

In short, according to Mr. Mitchell, two problems need to be solved before the world goes all electric. Both are eminently practical. The first is that the electric car has to be affordable for most people before more traditional options become obsolete. That means battery technology is going to have to be revolutionized. It's certainly possible. Henry Ford did in fact bring the price point for a car to a level that drove the horse and buggy into obsolescence.

The second problem is the electricity itself. Where does it come from? How is it generated? And then, how is it transported? We'll need a massively expanded grid capacity to handle the electricity necessary to power millions of new cars. It does raise some questions. Mr. Mitchell concludes:

If we're all flying around in jetpacks, then we're going to need fewer roads. But that's not necessarily going to be the case, particularly for the freight part of our work. And of course, we're all Americans

that like our freedom. We want to be able to drive where we want
when we want. For those who want to take a train, you still have
the last mile conversation. You can take a train to the town you
live in, but you're going to drive to your house. And so, how you're
going to do that is going to be different, but it's going to take a
road for a long, long time.

Our industry just needs to keep an open mind as to what that's
going to look like. It may be that our industry has to be the one to
change, but it also could be that our industry is going to be the one
that leads, because there's lots of really, really good things about our
product. We are the most recycled products in the world. And we
are 100 percent recyclable. We have reduced our energy consumption throughout our product and process over the last 10 years.
I believe and are going to keep us in the game for a long time.

Based upon its expertise and the industry's commitment to
science and innovation, NAPA is in conversation with the industry
about the future and how it might explore asphalt binder alternatives
in earnest.

Conclusion

The future offers no guarantees or promises for anyone; it never has,
and it never will. For the asphalt pavement industry that's never been
a problem. Steeped in its own strategic partnerships throughout its
supply chain, and uniting the industry through its strategic partner,
the NAPA, this industry is decidedly well positioned and prepared to
address whatever might come next.

As the industry's focal point, NAPA is an influential and effective
resource that attracts new partnerships, provides critical resources

and support to its members, and maintains and grows relationships on behalf of the industry. The trade association also effectively reinforces its partnerships with state asphalt pavement associations and all key stakeholders. The asphalt industry and NAPA strategic partnership is highly functional. Each reflects one another's values, and they are powered by innovation, data, science, and relationships. Their attributes were on full display as the industry and NAPA collaborated over the course of the last year to increase member engagement and strengthen the industry's grassroots network through a more streamlined governance structure at the trade association. Rather than become weighted down in an acrimonious debate, they used data and research to brainstorm and think through a volunteer framework that in the end will better serve and engage the industry. This speaks volumes about an industry always seeking to bring itself to the next level.

Jay Winford:

Here's what I feel from the heart. This is a wonderful, wonderful industry. And I'll even throw the concrete people with us. They pave roads, too. And the people that crush rocks. These guys built America. And until we have drones that can carry 400 pounds, and levitating cars, and all that, we have to have infrastructure. And let's define it the old-fashioned way of roads, bridges, ditches, the standard stuff, and water and wastewater systems to keep us safe and get us from point A to B.

In summing up, constructing pavement one lane at a time is a lot like building strategic partnerships. Both rely heavily upon bringing together the essential attributes of trust, expertise, doing the right thing, and community focus. In a time of increasing uncertainty and change, the asphalt pavement industry and NAPA show us how a strategic partnership helps an industry become more durable and flexible enough to address its challenges and even pave its own way to new opportunities.

7 Frozen Foods

People have been freezing food as a means of preservation and storage for a very long time. The modern frozen food industry, however, didn't officially begin until biologist, inventor, and entrepreneur Clarence Birdseye determined to make it so. In 1922, he "set out to 'create an industry, to find a commercially viable way of producing large quantities of fast frozen fish.'"[1]

In 1927, Birdseye invented a multiplate freezing machine to flash-freeze (or "quick-freeze,"[2] as he called it) haddock, a process he had witnessed among the Inuits while fur trading in Labrador more than a decade earlier. He pronounced it "a marvelous new process which seals in every bit of just-from-the-ocean flavor,"[3] and a brand-new industry was born.

By 1929, the great barrier to the success of Birdseye's nascent frozen food industry—public acceptance—was breached when General Foods arrived on the scene.[4] Today, frozen food is one of the fastest-growing categories in the food industry.

In 2019, the global frozen food market was valued at $291.8 billion.[5] The industry ecosystem is divided into two main components, *foodservice* and *retail*. See Figure 7.1.

Foodservice makes up the bulk of the frozen food industry; it includes everything from agriculture (the growing and production

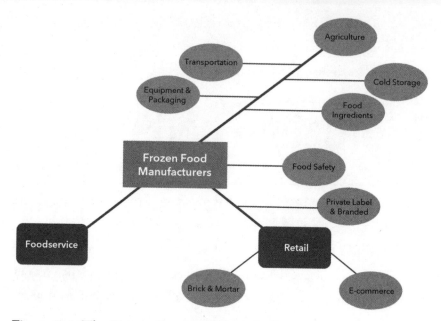

Figure 7.1 The Frozen Food Industry Ecosystem
Source: Illustration artwork prepared by Erin Wagner, Edge Research.

of the food), manufacturing (including the equipment needed for cleaning, peeling, chopping, and prepping prior to freezing, and other equipment necessary to get and keep food at a low-temperature state), packaging, cold warehousing, and transportation to anywhere and everywhere that provides meals or snacks to people outside their home, restaurants (midscale, fast casual, casual dining, quick-service retail, and fine dining) vs. institutional dining (K–12 schools, health-care, colleges and universities, lodging, business and industry), and even airlines, vending machines, and ice cream trucks.

Retail sales accounted for nearly $57 billion in 2018.[6] Two years later, in 2020 (in the midst of the pandemic), frozen food retail sales reached $65.1 billion.[7] The retail frozen food market has been on an upward trajectory since 2016 as the sector has been making a concerted effort to provide a wider variety of innovative frozen food offerings to satisfy evolving consumer needs and desires. We shall discuss this in some detail presently.

Some of the larger companies that play a substantial role in frozen food include General Mills, Inc., J.R. Simplot Co., Cargill, Nestlé, Tyson Foods, Ajinomoto, Kraft Heinz Co., ConAgra Foods, Inc., McCain Foods, Nomad Foods Ltd., Wawona Frozen Foods, and Unilever.

Food Matters

As we all know, food matters. Everyone eats. Food touches everyone's life. It is a physiological necessity. It sits at the base level of Maslow's Hierarchy of Needs pyramid. Without it we would all perish from this earth. But food is not just about sustenance and nourishment. It's much more than just a physiological need. Food is so important, so personal, so much a part of our lives. We give food to our children and to those we care about most; it's something around which we celebrate and around which we make memories.

One could argue that food fits meaningfully into at least four of Maslow's five levels of motivation (see Figure 7.2):

- Physiological
- Safety: Consider how people—and governments—stockpile food in times of fear or crisis (one need only recall the early days of the recent pandemic; but consider also the victory gardens of World War II and rationing during natural disaster response).
- Love/belonging: Think about the importance of food in the celebration of holidays (Easter eggs and chocolates, Fourth of July

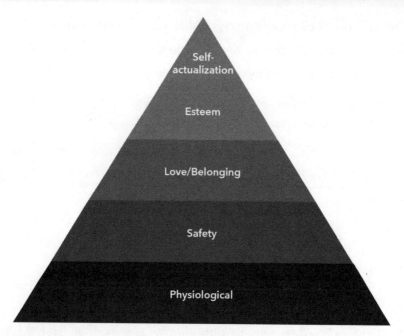

Figure 7.2 Maslow's Hierarchy of Needs
Source: Illustration artwork prepared by Erin Wagner, Edge Research.

barbecues, Thanksgiving turkeys, perhaps the Christmas goose), family reunions and social gatherings (the picnic, the fish fry, the church potluck; parties of every description, and for any reason), and simple family meals or intimate dinner parties with friends.

• Esteem: Remember the banquets you've attended to honor and celebrate great people and great achievements; wedding receptions and funeral repasts, graduation parties and retirement dinners. The list goes on.

The importance of food to humans is existential in its broadest sense. I think because of that fact many of the people involved in the food business (and particularly in the frozen food industry, at least in my experience) seem to share certain values that center around relationships. They tend to value family, honesty, trust, integrity, and transparency. They care about people: their employees, their co-workers, and their customers. They care about keeping people safe, and healthy, and delighted. They talk freely and animatedly about food safety, and sustainability, recyclable packaging, reducing food waste, and protecting the environment. And the same is true of the companies they found or build or join.

The American Frozen Food Institute (AFFI)

As I have said before (hopefully without belaboring the point), the trade associations that represent industries generally share the values of those industries they serve and represent. In turn, the industries that passionately value their customers, their relationships, and their business frequently flourish, in no small part because they are usually pretty good at forming and maintaining strong and fruitful strategic partnerships.

AFFI is no exception to the rule. Indeed, AFFI is a mirror image of the frozen food industry, in its values, objectives, and outcomes. And because of it, AFFI and the frozen food industry are forging a powerful and effectual strategic partnership.

The CEO and president of AFFI, Alison Bodor, is an excellent example of how this works. Alison is a thoughtful, smart, strategic, energetic, and extremely talented leader. She is passionate about the frozen food industry, laser-focused on its unique value proposition, driven by science and data, and utterly devoted to the partnerships, alliances, and relationships that move the industry successfully into the future. In my opinion, it is not too much to say that she and her team at AFFI are the face of the frozen food industry, at least in Washington.

Frozen Food Industry Value Proposition 1: Laser Focus

There truly is an association for everything and there are a slew of associations that represent different sectors of the vast food economy. And many of these associations represent businesses and business issues that are important to AFFI's members. One thinks of the National Association of Manufacturers (NAM), or the Chamber of Commerce, or Consumer Brands Association (CBA), or FMI - The Food Industry Association, among dozens of others. In Ms. Bodor's estimation, AFFI delivers value to its members precisely because it is exclusively focused on frozen food. That is its role. It's why AFFI exist. It's what AFFI does.

When she joined AFFI in 2016, Ms. Bodor committed to both the association and the industry to be hyperfocused always and entirely on frozen. The primary criteria AFFI uses to decide where to engage—where to commit time, energy, and resources—are (1) how important and impactful the problem or opportunity is to frozen, and (2) how unique it is to frozen. Not all issues that are impactful to frozen are unique to frozen. That, she says, is where AFFI starts to manage their issues and manage what they do so that they will always take the lead on those issues that are both unique to frozen and have high impact on frozen. That's where they can impact an issue and deliver value.

AFFI members sell all kinds of foods in a frozen temperature state. They sell everything from fruits and vegetables to meat and poultry; from breakfast foods and appetizers and soups and entrees to cakes and pies and ice cream. You name it, they sell it into retail and/or foodservice. In theory, therefore, AFFI could legitimately get involved in every issue affecting food. But if they were to do that, it would be duplicating resources with other associations that are involved in food.

For issues that are impactful to frozen but are not unique to frozen, AFFI looks to its trade association peers to take the lead. It will be supportive, and will often help out, but it doesn't spend significant time or resources there. Ms. Bodor commented thus: "We take those relationships with our peer associations very seriously. I do and so does my staff. One of the core values that's ingrained in us is that we are honest, credible partners with the folks that we work with."

She sums up AFFI's value proposition like this: "We are not going to duplicate efforts with other associations. We remain nimble and flexible to pivot as needed, as the issues demand, but we are not going to lose sight of why we're here. We're here because our members sell foods at a certain temperature state." Frozen.

Frozen Food Industry Value Proposition 2: Primacy of Science

Another unique aspect that differentiates AFFI from other associations is that it is always and intentionally "driven by the science." One of the core strengths of the association, says Ms. Bodor (whose undergraduate degree is a BS in food science from Cornell), "[is the fact that] we have a strong scientific bench in our employee base, and we leverage that." It's how AFFI routinely approaches issues. "What is the science behind the issue, or how can we use science to help us achieve the outcome?" asks Ms. Bodor. "We've done that with every issue that we've worked on, whether it's grappling with the scientific and regulatory affairs of food safety, or addressing communications issues in our industry, or concentrating on category growth and looking at consumer insights, or confronting the future of sustainability and e-commerce. What is the data that's going to lead our industry? We ask ourselves. And then that's going to lead us to find the right partners."

John Tentomas, founder and chief executive of Nature's Touch Frozen Foods, had this to say on the subject: "I think [it's] a natural advantage of the association, probably its biggest strength today. Nobody's going to question the technical capabilities of AFFI . . . It's by far their biggest core strength." He regards AFFI's science-based assessments and recommendations as unimpeachable.

Meghan Swan, who serves as vice president for McDonald's Global Business, J.R. Simplot Company (which, incidentally, means her job is to help ensure they continue to deliver on the gold standard of French fries), echoes the sentiment: "AFFI's science-based approached gives so much credibility to how we represent ourselves as an industry. Their understanding of how we need to focus in on research and prove out our business cases before we try to execute on something has been transformational in the association in terms of people's buy-in on what the strategies are, and where we're going to invest the dollars that we are pooling together as an industry."

Frozen Food Industry Value Proposition 3: Shared Values

As I mentioned, AFFI reflects the values of the frozen food industry. In my view, one of the most compelling values within the industry (which I alluded to earlier) is that the overriding culture is very much like a family. Its charm for me lies in the unusual mixture of progressive ideas and plain, almost old-fashioned goodness. Allow me to illustrate what I mean with a couple of stories and comments told to me by AFFI members.

"Keep Sawing Wood"

Julia Sabin is the vice president of government relations and corporate sustainability at the J.M. Smucker Co., also known as Smucker. After completing a BS in biochemistry at UCLA, she returned to her hometown of Chico, California, got married, and went to work for a small juice company. Smucker bought that little company a year later, and she has stayed with them for her entire 37-year career. Smucker is a publicly traded company that was founded in 1897.

In 1994, Ms. Sabin raised her hand and asked if she could be a plant manager. It was outside her wheelhouse, but the leadership knew her, trusted her, and agreed to take a chance on her. It was a risk. She was Californian, she was a young wife and mother, and she was being uprooted and moved across the country to northwestern Pennsylvania to take over a food plant, a job that in those days was done exclusively by men. It was hard. There were plenty of challenges, as one can easily imagine. But the company believed in her. They stood by her. One of her most vivid memories from that experience was being told by third-generation CEO Paul Smucker, "All you have to do is keep sawing wood. If you keep sawing wood, the tree will come down." It worked. She persevered. And she excelled as a leader.

The next opportunity for advancement was a little further beyond Ms. Sabin's experience, training, and expertise. She was nervous about a new role. She remembers sharing her apprehension with Tim Smucker, mentioning particularly that she had not finished her master's (which she'd intended to do). His response was life-giving: "Stop," he said. "Stop. You have everything you need to be successful with our company. And we won't let you fail." Tremendous relief flooded over her; a heavy burden just dropped from her shoulders. She told me that she changed as a person overnight in terms of confidence and courage, knowing that she could push the edge of the envelope, be creative, and get out there and say what she thinks. And from that moment on, that's what she did.

"A Little Less Progressive"

Meghan Swan told me she was initially attracted to J.R. Simplot Company because of its values and culture. Here's what she had to say on the matter:

> It's a family-owned business. It feels like a small business even though it's a global, multibillion-dollar business. The number one reason people say they want to join the company or like working here is the people. They love working with the people throughout the organization.
>
> Agribusiness can be a bit less progressive than other industries. When I first went to AFFI I noticed I was the only woman in the room besides Ali [Alison Bodor] and her staff members. There was also a large demographic gap within the age range when I first came in. Over time that has changed.
>
> It always felt like there was such a deep, deep friendship among the member companies. As generations have evolved, as the way we do business has evolved, it's harder to have that depth of relationship. Ali has gone to great lengths to create that sense of community alignment, build those relationships, build that level of trust. And COVID made it a million times harder as we were trying to do it all virtually.
>
> AFFI feels like our company in that it is all about the people. It's about understanding the true business needs. It's about

authenticity, and being real with each other, and up front. But it's also this ability to feel like we are making a true change within the industry, and it's about innovation, which is core to how we see ourselves at Simplot. It's about continuous improvement, innovating for the future, and planning for the longer term.

Alison Bodor is taking time to get to know us, understand our businesses, what our challenges are so she can relate that to the whole. It is all about relationships for her.

AFFI's Priority Issues and the Relationships They Cultivate: Past, Present, and Future

By focusing on science and data, and by holding to the highest standards of honesty, integrity, and transparency, AFFI—esteemed strategic partner to the frozen food industry—has also built strong strategic relationships with scientists and universities, federal regulators, and peer trade associations to successfully extend their reach, meet challenges, and pursue opportunities. The most prominent among these in the past and present (and no doubt going forward) are advancing food safety and category growth (i.e., the expansion of frozen food as a percentage of the broader food industry). Another subject being discussed currently, because it is so recent and so raw and possibly not yet entirely over, is the COVID-19 pandemic and AFFI's response to it. Two of the hottest topics today and looking to the future are sustainability and e-commerce. Let's have a look at each of these.

Food Safety

Advancing food safety has been the frozen food industry's priority ever since Clarence Birdseye set out to show the world that flash-freezing fish filets (and other foods) keeps them safe over time, without preservatives. Alison Bodor joined AFFI right when there was a major recall of frozen foods due to a pathogen called *Listeria mono-cytogenes*. Listeria is an unusual pathogen in that it survives freezing temperatures, so it is a perennial concern in the frozen food industry. Ms. Bodor immediately embarked on a strategic planning process for the industry, and the board prioritized the advancement of food safety within the frozen food industry supply chain. Alison Bodor and her uniquely qualified team doubled down on food safety and made it their signature strength. "We knew then that AFFI could be instrumental to both our members and the collective frozen food industry by developing the science and best practices to ensure that frozen foods and beverages are safe," noted Ms. Bodor.

To combat the risk of the pathogen, AFFI created a comprehensive strategy to develop the science to understand the pathogen risk in frozen foods and to create a set of best practices for the industry to mitigate the pathogen in frozen food manufacturing. The organization on behalf of the industry committed to sharing the best practices and science with regulatory agencies to advance policies that would ensure public health.

John Tentomas, whose company is Canadian, takes up the narrative: "Over the past several years, the frozen food industry has experienced some unique food safety challenges. The number one concern if you're dealing in food, and you're dealing in ready-to-eat food, is food safety. No one wants a consumer to get sick. The liability environment in the U.S. is so intense that you have to think twice about even trying to attempt to come into this market as a new player."

Mr. Tentomas described the United States as "a regulatory-rich environment. It's incredibly complicated, and the guidelines are not always clear. You need help," he assured me. AFFI helped open up the U.S. market for Nature's Touch, "maybe more efficiently than having to acquire a business" already operating in the United States. It is true that many companies today enter the U.S. market by acquisition.

"Where there are food safety issues that are unique to frozen and high-impact," Ms. Bodor told me, "we jumped in and created fulsome strategies around those concerns." She continued, "We look for an industry approach and a regulatory approach to manage food safety issues that will improve public health, and do it in a way that allows companies to manage the issues in a practical and achievable and cost-effective manner. And we look to the science to help us drive that."

AFFI has partnered with scientists, universities, and the academic community generally to advance food safety. In fact, they have a scientific advisory committee made up of world-renowned scientists from a number of universities. And experts are often engaged ad hoc, based on the nature of the problem at hand. On pathogen controls, for example, AFFI has worked with the University of Georgia, Cornell University, and the University of Minnesota and engaged global experts in Europe and South America. They've worked on nutrition with the University of Georgia and the University of California, Davis.

According to Ms. Bodor:

We've funded research that in the past the regulatory agencies would probably have done themselves. But in today's environment, with tight budgets, it's really challenging for them to do so. And so, we've made those investments. They are expensive, long-term, visionary investments that can be tough for an industry and nearly impossible for a single company to do on their own. But it's a perfect example of how companies can come together and invest collaboratively to improve an industry.

The academic community partners with us, often donating their time to our efforts because they share our passion for advancing food safety in a way that will improve public health in the short term, but also provide the industry with new tools to continuously improve public health into the future. It's how we drive innovation, frankly, in food safety: through working with our academic partners, industry experts, and suppliers of food safety services. And because we have a reputation for being honest brokers of science, external scientists are comfortable working with industry under the AFFI banner.

And that strategy of advancing food safety in partnership with the academic community has helped us build relationships with the regulatory agencies. We approach regulatory agencies with the science and data in hand. And if we need more data, we'll go get it. If we need outside expertise—because we don't have it all in house, of course—we'll go get that, too.

The regulatory agencies, chiefly the FDA and the [United States Department of Agriculture] USDA, recognize our credibility, appreciate our data, and are open to considering our suggestions and approaches.

Of course, AFFI doesn't necessarily win every time. And the regulatory agencies don't necessarily agree with them every time. But they do know that AFFI will always bring real and credible solutions to the table. And they know that any pushback is not an obstinate no to regulation. Instead, it is a "yes, and we have an alternative way that may be better for both public health and also better for our members," Ms. Bodor states.

John Tentomas describes AFFI's extraordinary contribution toward managing the risk of *Listeria monocytogenes* and, more recently, enteric viruses this way: "AFFI created a recipe book for having a 100 percent FDA regulatory compliant plant. And it's incredible."

I asked Mr. Tentomas, from the perspective of a leading retail provider of frozen fruit, to share a more detailed account of how AFFI has more recently engaged the supply chain of frozen fruit to mitigate risks of enteric viruses on fruits. Some imported frozen fruits are grown in areas of the world where hepatitis A is endemic and unsafe water supplies exist, so harvesting the berries by hand can create opportunities for the virus to transfer to the fruit. In those areas, it's especially important that good agricultural practices, especially frequent hand washing, are used to prevent the virus from contacting the fruit.

Mr. Tentomas shared that around 2018 the FDA began a surveillance program of enteric viruses in frozen berries that resulted in several recalls. "That really shook the industry. Thankfully, AFFI was there. Their team immediately engaged the frozen fruit suppliers and the FDA and quickly noted that gaps in the science exist around testing and understanding the true risk to public health."

AFFI gathered global experts in viral science, many of whom are now actively engaged in COVID-19 research, and asked them to provide input on appropriate testing methodologies and how to use test results to assess risk of foodborne viral illness. AFFI plans to publish the work of this expert panel to make it available to regulatory and public health agencies globally.

Additionally, AFFI worked with its member companies to develop best practices that could be leveraged across the frozen fruit supply chain to encourage suppliers around the world to adopt best food safety practices.

I asked Mr. Tentomas to share a more detailed account of how AFFI's leadership on frozen fruit safety has benefited his company. Tentomas himself reported participating in the development of the best practices and contributed to the "recipe book" approach to managing this potential viral risk just as AFFI had done with other pathogens. "It's based on the simple idea that what's good for the company is good for the industry, and vice versa. And what's best for the consumer is best for everyone involved."

Mr. Tentomas said the advantage to Nature's Touch is that "once an association comes up with best practices that are validated by experts, not just by one or two industry peers, it creates a new and higher standard that not only levels the competitive playing field but, more importantly, improves the food safety profile for consumers."

Alison Bodor summed up her thoughts on working with the scientific community, regulatory agencies, and the frozen food industry to improve food safety and thus protect the growth of the frozen food category:

> In food safety, we must use science to drive policy and industry practices. AFFI relies on good science to characterize risk and inform strategies in our supply chain and within our frozen food facilities to lower risks. If we don't produce safe food, we won't have food to sell. This industry is steadfastly supportive of advancements in food safety and that's good because it's a journey without end.
>
> There's always more we can do. And we need our partners in the scientific community to help us conduct the best research. And we need our industry experts to participate in the research too and then determine how to operationalize the findings. And we need honest, transparent, and credible interactions with regulatory

agencies since we all have the same goal of ensuring public health. I'm proud that AFFI is delivering on all these fronts.

Category Growth: The Power of Frozen

Several years ago, AFFI and FMI - The Food Industry Association, which represents food retailers (grocery companies), formalized a strategic partnership to kick off a joint initiative they called the *Power of Frozen*. Their shared objective was to reset the conversation around the frozen food category by doing in-depth market research, collecting retail sales data—overlaying that with consumer trends and identifying opportunities for both retailers' and manufacturers' strategies to expand the frozen food industry.

The first major research and data collection was accomplished in 2018. The study essentially combined IRI retail purchasing data with survey research designed to collect primary data from consumers, evaluating their consumption, purchase drivers, and use of frozen foods. The data was shared with FMI and AFFI members in 2019 in the first *Power of Frozen* report. They shared this primary consumer data with the entire food industry so that all stakeholders would appreciate what was happening in the category.

Two discoveries were of special interest to AFFI:

1. Consumer interest in the frozen category was already in the midst of a revival. In 2018, both dollar (+2.6 percent) and units (2.3 percent) grew, with 9 out of 10 top-selling categories up in dollars and all 10 up in units. The landscape was already improving markedly.

2. The data had zeroed in on the core frozen-food consumer, which turned out to be an older millennial, working, with children.

A tremendous amount of innovation was already being done in the frozen category over the 2015–2017 time frame. Companies had completely revamped product, streamlined ingredient declarations, and modernized the category to suit consumers' needs, especially around quality, taste, variety, and health.

Julia Sabin had this to say: "Perception is everything sometimes. Five years ago, the frozen aisle was TV dinners and bags of peas. Today, it's foodie. It's gourmet, it's healthy. It's protein power lunches. It's got splurge items."

"Innovation was the driver," Ms. Sabin remarked. She mentioned Smucker's Uncrustables®, which are Smucker's only foray as yet into the frozen world. With a sly grin, she asked, "What, you can't make your own peanut butter sandwich?" But she quickly pointed out that the modern family wants convenience. People are busy, they're working, they're raising a family. "Frozen just innovated at the right time," she told me. "On the taste profile (and taste is always king), the quality, the price, convenience: Frozen delivered." She also made it a point to remind me that with regard to retailers, "What's good for us is good for them."

AFFI was now equipped with valuable data about what was happening in the industry, what consumers were looking for, and what trends were unfolding. They were then able to use that information effectively in dealing with both the business media and consumer media to share the benefits and business of frozen. This allowed AFFI to articulate how those benefits are translating into sales.

Ms. Bodor told the story of the meteoric rise of frozen during the pandemic:

The frozen category had already begun to pick up noticeably in 2017 and 2018. And the same again in 2019. And then

COVID-19 hit. Frozen was the right food at the right time during the pandemic. Consumers were looking to reduce their grocery store trips. People were at home, preparing three meals a day. That's a lot of time in the kitchen when you're trying to balance home life and your job while your kids are also at home doing school on the computer. It was a lot to juggle. Frozen meals were a real solution for working parents especially. Frozen gave consumers the convenience, comfort, variety, and healthiness that consumers were seeking.

And as the consumer demands healthier foods, frozen food companies are delivering options including plant-based proteins, whole grains, high-fiber, low-sodium, low-fat, organic, GMO-free, and portion-controlled foods.

Of course, the frozen aisle also offers more indulgent foods like frozen pizza, stuffed potato skins, and cherry pie that are fun foods we all enjoy in our diet.

And so, we saw that growth extend by over 20 percent during the pandemic. We brought new consumers to the category. And we also increased our interaction, our engagement with the consumer across all meal solutions. That growth is a silver lining for the frozen food industry from this horrible pandemic. Our goal as an industry is to keep the consumers who discovered frozen foods during COVID and to maintain the increased engagement by our core millennial consumers.

The frozen category is well-positioned for growth moving forward. Millennials are just starting families and ramping up that very busy phase of life of balancing work with home responsibilities, so we expect they will continue to turn to frozen. Even as consumers begin to return to restaurants as COVID recedes, we're still seeing more growth in frozen than in other grocery categories.

There is still a great deal of work to be done in communicating the innovations and expansion of frozen foods that are now available. It's a bit of a chicken-and-egg problem. Retailers need to be convinced to expand their frozen aisles to provide more space to accommodate the influx of new frozen products. But to do that, consumers need to know that these new products exist, and demand them from the retailers. It's going to require focused effort.

John Tentomas is intrigued by the topic and speaks passionately about it:

> We as an industry have been playing a lot of defense. We need to do some offense. Frozen was considered the place for ice cream and pizza and French fries. Then veggies to a certain degree. Then fruit. And so on. The healthier options have created a renewed vigor in the frozen food industry more than anything.

> Freezer space has not grown significantly in retailers, so frozen is extremely competitive. And it's a zero-sum game. Whatever you put in there, something has to come out. It's no longer just TV dinners. Now there are healthy, tasty, exotic options. And even with indulgences. There are exotic flavors for ice cream, there is now lactose free, there is plant-based. There are all these new choices. But not much new space.

> My objective is to find mediums by which we can provide consumers with more choice. Today we are literally handcuffed by limited space at grocery stores. Aldi and Trader Joe's are exceptions as the percentage of footprint for the frozen market is very high at those retailers. And there's a reason for that. Obviously, they understand it. But most grocery stores have maybe two aisles of frozen.

Traditional channel management related to frozen certainly does present a challenge, but perhaps it's a good problem to have. The market is clearly moving in favor of frozen on a number of fronts. And AFFI's close alliance with FMI will certainly provide access and assistance in spreading the word through retailers that frozen is on the march. Providing fact-based information through the *Power of Frozen* could drive retailers to invest in the assets necessary to expand retail space for frozen. A united front, intentional collaboration, strategic communication, and a strong strategic partnership could assuredly move the needle for the industry.

COVID-19 Pandemic Response

The strategic partnership between AFFI and the industry (as represented by AFFI's own board of directors) was cemented as a result of the pandemic. Members of both the executive committee and the board have indicated that they relied heavily on AFFI when COVID-19 hit. They wanted to know how things were going to change with respect to regulations, they wanted to know how they could keep their workers safe and secure, and they wanted to know what they needed to do as an industry. It was, at least initially, all frozen all the time, 24/7. And AFFI stepped up and became the eyes and ears of the industry to help the industry navigate through those difficult challenges.

Alison Bodor tells the story this way:

The first thing AFFI did at the outset was connect with our peer associations in the nation's capital. The food industry associations circled the wagons to be intentional in how we protected

the ability of our manufacturers to operate. We held regular
conversations, every day of the week in the early days, to figure
out what we were facing, and how it was going to affect our food
supply. Of course, it was not unique to frozen food, but it was
massively impactful to all food. The entire food industry needed
to work together to understand the full breadth of the impact,
and also to understand what solutions we might have as a united
force. We understood that we would be more effective working
together than individually.

It was an unprecedented situation. All of a sudden, government
agencies that lack deep knowledge of the food industry were creating (or not creating, as the case may be) policies that were impacting the food industry at a point in time when the companies that
the associations represented were working 24 hours a day to stay
operational to continue to put food on American tables.

That partnership among the food associations was vital in getting
the food industry designated as part of the critical infrastructure
of our nation. That designation was mission critical to ensure that
companies could get supplies across state lines and that employees
could get to work when cities were shutting down.

Julia Sabin described the situation from the member company
frame of reference:

When COVID hit, we were scrambling to figure out how to keep
our manufacturing employees safe. In a frozen food manufacturing
factory, employees sometimes work really close together physically, for
long hours.

We had to figure out what was going on with this pandemic.
We knew we had to figure out a way to keep the plants running, or

we wouldn't be feeding Americans. That sounds a little bodacious, but that's how our employees felt.

All our leaders were grappling with how we were going to handle it all. We had our quality people, we had our human resources, we had our OSHA experts. We had everybody trying to figure this out. It was AFFI that stepped up. And I genuinely mean that.

My team and I recognized we needed our employees classified as essential workers. We understood that medical personnel were the top priority, but we were right up there, too. The demand was over the top for certain products because people were at home in lockdown and couldn't go out.

AFFI stepped up and wrote the language and organized the associations early on to advocate to the federal government that the food industry workers should be considered "essential workers." It was a team effort across the food industry, but if AFFI had not played the initial leadership role they did, we wouldn't have gotten that designation so quickly.

AFFI also provided guidance to their member companies on how to protect their workers. What personal protective equipment (PPE) was required? What physical distance or barrier was needed between workers and under what conditions? Was it necessary to wear masks? And if so, where do companies get masks? How should companies handle sick workers? How do companies put these recommendations into action in their facilities? All of those and many more questions were being asked and quick answers were critical.

In the early days, AFFI was creating guidance and providing resources for their members when guidance didn't exist from regulatory agencies. As Bodor explained, "AFFI's expert staff developed guidance with some of their peers in the industry and at other associations. And we got that information to our members before the government did. That was huge and it saved lives. I am 100 percent certain that our members saved lives because of the work that we did collectively on worker safety."

The supply chain was breaking down on the food service side of the house as restaurants closed almost overnight. At the same time, it was challenging to keep up with demand for food at grocery stores. AFFI became a liaison between the frozen food industry and the White House's Task Force on Coronavirus and the regulatory agencies with oversight of food. AFFI, in partnership with its food association peers, was the voice of the industry and conveyed their needs to government, seeking solutions to worker safety and supply chain disruptions, access to critical personal protective equipment, and ultimately access to vaccines.

The information was coming in fast and furious, and evolving daily. We made it our job to be the filter for our members, and to curate that data as it came in; to streamline it, summarize it, make it easily accessible, and get it out to our members in a timely fashion. We were sending out a newsletter three times a week—Monday, Wednesday, and Friday—early on, and sometimes with alerts in between. That curated information saved our members time and gave them what was most relevant and most important in an easily digestible format.

It really was an extraordinary effort in extraordinary times. And it just goes to show the importance and value of an authentic strategic partner. They're sometimes quite literally worth their weight in gold.

Sustainability

Sustainability is a very important topic in food and agriculture. And it matters more than just a little bit to the millennial generation, frozen food's core customer base.

AFFI is in the process right now of understanding what their stakeholders expect of the frozen category with regard to sustainability. Once they have got that figured out, they are going to have to work out how to deliver on those expectations. Ms. Bodor expects that food waste and possibly energy use will top the list of what matters.

As it turns out, frozen food is a solution for food waste on the consumer side. While food waste occurs throughout the value chain of food production from farm to fork, approximately 40 percent occurs at home. According to a study done in the UK, frozen foods generate 47% less food waste when compared to ambient and chilled food consumed at home.[8] It is an opportunity for AFFI and the industry to communicate how frozen foods can help reduce overall food waste. As Ms. Bodor points out, "There's never been more talk about food waste than there is right now. So, making sure we've got the right data and messaging on food waste is another way we can align as an industry."

John Tentomas wonders what role frozen plays "in this sustainability-rich dialogue environment today in terms of how consumers are looking at food and their impact on the environment and the players that are involved in that environment." He feels that "defining the frozen narrative" is going to be important in relation to food waste, convenience, local versus international, and the carbon footprint between these two areas. "There's a certain advantage in preservation in frozen," Mr. Tentomas notes, "that believe it or not saves a lot of carbon at the end of the day. So clearly identifying that value proposition and telling both retailers and consumers about it will drive increased traffic to the frozen section and move it forward."

The industry must identify what needs to be done in order to be considered sustainability stewards for the category. Many companies are doing it already, and many have stated objectives and goals about how they will improve:

- Packaging
- Energy use
- Water use
- Employee fairness
- Equity
- Social awareness and social capital

Many of the larger companies are already well down the path of figuring out what sustainability means to their customers and stakeholders. They have to be. Retailers are demanding it of them.

Mr. Tentomas believes packaging may end up being one of the major issues. "The frozen food industry definitely has plastics challenges. There's no question. Maybe the answer is to come up with an industry approach towards frozen packaging materials to make sure that they're more sustainable."

Julia Sabin remembers Smucker's thinking about sustainability issues long before the term was even known, let alone fashionable. She remembers their "work in that area goes back to installing solar panels and recycling everything at our Chico facility, which was organic and all-natural, back in the 1980s."

E-Commerce

"E-commerce is the wave of the future," Ms. Bodor told me. "It's not going away." She wonders whether brick-and-mortar will even exist in the next quarter century. "It will be here," she concedes, "but e-commerce is going to take a bigger and bigger share of the overall grocery bill."

She wants to make sure that frozen takes full advantage of the growth of e-commerce. She notes that "there are some particularly unique challenges to frozen in multiple aspects of e-commerce. Those are perfect areas for us to delve into. They are not unique to all foods; they are unique to frozen. So that's what we're going to double down on, e-commerce."

Ms. Bodor had this to say on the subject of e-commerce:

We're still pretty early in those conversations. There are some intersections around food safety that are right in our sweet spot in terms of that last mile of delivery, making sure that the quality and safety of the food is there for the consumer regardless of the mechanism of commerce.

And what is the role of frozen in working with retailers on click-and-collect programs? What is the role of frozen working with other partners on direct-to-consumer e-commerce?

Companies are just getting started in direct-to-consumer programs. Across the topic of e-commerce, there's an opportunity to bring companies together for joint learning and to figure out solutions.

From an association standpoint, our challenge in e-commerce is making sure that we find opportunities and/or hurdles that are pre-competitive in nature. Because that's where associations work best.

If we find ourselves in a competitive space, then we won't be successful. In e-commerce right now we're assessing which unique
frozen food barriers or opportunities are pre-competitive in nature
and which would benefit most from industry collaboration.

John Tentomas spoke at some length on the subject:

E-commerce will possibly allow us not only to expand the options
for consumers, but also maybe even improve upon the quality of
the product that consumers receive at their door versus the traditional way of buying frozen food, which is going to the grocery
store and then bringing it to your house.

Changes in temperature through the entire traditional process and
the whole supply chain before even getting to the retailer present
some challenges. There [are] a lot of temperature variances because
a lot of handling is going on, which causes at least visual degra-
dation of the product prior to the consumer using it.

If you live in Florida, for example (or anywhere on a hot summer day in the U.S.), and you buy anything frozen, including ice
cream, then you go home and put it back in the freezer, what happens to it? It becomes like ice. It gets frosty. And it doesn't really
look or taste as good.

One of our big challenges compared to fresh is texture and appear-
ance. Well, I think we can make a really big dent in that handicap
by finding better ways of sending it to consumers in properly
temperature-controlled environments.

Today people find it conceptually difficult to understand how you
can ship a bag of peas to a house. But 15 years ago, no one thought
Amazon would deliver toilet paper to your door. Meanwhile, it's

competitive, and it's convenient, and it's happening. So obviously Amazon has built an infrastructure that has surpassed the traditional brick-and-mortar distribution modes and has figured out how to do the hub-and-spoke principle, straight to consumers' homes. And it has expanded the choice of consumers significantly in products that they never even thought was possible before.

We feel as an industry we need to find a way to do that, where we are not hindered by listing fees and shelf space and all the other encumbrances of traditional models. We need to find a way to provide for consumers more choice of frozen. That will provide more competition, which is also good for consumers, and it will open the door for food service and other kinds of players to participate as well.

And then there's the digital media marketing side of it that consumers can actually spend more time understanding products online—because they do that—rather than walking through a grocery store and taking a glance at a package, and therefore not really knowing the product.

Conclusion

The frozen food industry is growing. And it is changing all the time. Years from now leaders in the frozen food industry may look back at the pre- and post-COVID-19 timeframe as an inflection point. Consumer tastes were changing, baby boomers were no longer the dominant demographic, and millennials would come to rely on food sources that included more options that are tasteful, healthy, and safe choices for themselves and their families. Topline growth performance, while impressive during the pandemic, is still strong, showing double-digit growth post pandemic.

One of the key takeaways in strategic partnership comes down to leadership from the industry and its trade association. Frozen food industry leaders reflected deftness and fluidity in how they managed and connected with their consumers. AFFI aligned with the same characteristics but elevated its leadership for the industry at new and different levels. With Alison Bodor at the helm, the association established science as its baseline, built trust as a pathway forward, and applied data in every conversation among all its partners.

Data helps industries and regulators come together to have constructive conversations about food safety. And data helps this industry continue to innovate and find new and compelling ways to further cement its relationships with a growing base of consumers. The same dialogue will continue around the next frontier as AFFI is facilitating future and precompetitive discussions around sustainability and e-commerce.

Ms. Bodor and her team view their efforts as similar to the early innings in a baseball game. Applying the industry strategic plan as their roadmap, they will build upon their strong foundation:

- Grounded in science, mitigate risks to the frozen food business.
- Elevate frozen's voice and build champions to promote the benefits of frozen foods.
- Drive solutions for innovative category performance.

AFFI is poised to lead it well. Their commitment to industry and consumer values, their reliance on science and data, their integrity and transparency, and their unwavering devotion to relationships make them the ideal strategic partner for the frozen food industry.

8 Breakthrough Opportunities for Industries and Trade Associations

At a time when industries face new growth challenges, it is energizing to share such a compelling call to action for industry executives. The five case studies presented here document how other industry executives extend their reach far to shape the business environment through strategic partnerships with their trade associations. Each case study is supported with tangible examples and outcomes by executives and leaders. It is the strategic partnerships that fuel opportunities to reimagine industry growth. Fully engaged, the partnerships deliver quantifiable and accretive business solutions for the industries they serve.

Nowadays, there is a lot of conversation of what cannot be done. Many say we are in uncharted waters, and that is true. Others say that a longer-term cohesive industry growth strategy is not feasible. However, as I spoke directly with industry leaders and trade association executives and staff, they uncovered new and different thinking. Much of what they shared are viable and increasingly effective approaches to achieve durable growth, including well planned customer-centric strategic partnerships that employ strategic planning and scenario planning: they are effective, and they work. New ground is broken regularly from these and other strategic partnerships, but not all of them were able to be included in this book. As a CEO or C-level executive, you and your industry have opportunities to apply the principles immediately and to confidently begin your industry's journey forward.

I hope having read this book you will take away a new meaning and application of strategic partnerships. In their practical application, strategic partnerships are functional relationships that align in a precompetitive space to overcome the biggest challenges, and then brainstorm a go-forward strategic approach to shape a more favorable external business environment.

I have not discussed political leadership, political polarization, or economic cycles, and there is a reason for that. Undoubtedly, every election has consequences, sometimes severe in nature. New leaders in Washington, DC and in state capitols exert influence over policies and regulations that most definitely affect the way in which industries conduct business. And newly elected officials from members of Congress to state legislatures in many instances may fund new and shifting priorities. Since there will always be changes in political power and in economic cycles, I have tried here to help business executives take a step back and think in broader terms based more on fundamental human characteristics than on the shifts in cultural or political winds and the normal vicissitudes of life.

Think back to the start of the global pandemic; refer back to the baking industry and the food and beverage industry alliance and how they effectively leveraged their ecosystem to keep plants operating, to protect their workers, and to keep the American people fed. Or think about their ecosystem's efforts to protect the industry when the state of New Jersey wanted to shut down independent distributors. Also think about the frozen food industry, how they utilized their ecosystem to achieve historic growth prepandemic and explosive growth during and postpandemic. Both industries functioned in different political environments at the federal and state levels of government.

The strategic partner strategy with your industry trade association can work as it has in other industries. In moving forward, your industry can become more fluid and flexible in its approaches and still be able to have the broadest impact in shaping the external environment. Factually, the five industries I wrote about rarely miss a beat because of their trade association strategic partnerships. In each, their ecosystems provide them the range and the reach to innovate, become more efficient as an industry, and make effective cases to regulators and legislators, as necessary. In a dramatic period of uncertainty, this is an approach worth pursuing.

Corporate Executives: Trade Associations Are Ready for Strategic Partnerships

I am confident that every corporate executive wonders if the timing is right to move forward with their trade association strategic partnerships. In fact, they are and enthusiastically so. COVID-19 and rapid innovation are transforming trade associations into the front porch for industries. Trade association executives see the shifts and are ready to move with their industry. The pre- and postpandemic timeframe shows how significant the role of trade associations has become for the industries they serve.

Think back to the recreational boating industry and how they leveraged their ecosystem to engage consumers on lockdown to explore and enjoy outdoor recreation. Boating sales skyrocketed. For that matter, so did sales of bicycles and motorcycles, RVs and ATVs, kayaks, windsurfers and canoes, and literally every type of equipment designed to enhance the pleasure of the great outdoors. It is clearer today that industry trade associations are ready. They recognize how they have become the face of their industry. And they can play an unmistakable role in overcoming impediments, shaping the external environment, and assisting with the achievement of long-term growth for their industry.

The time is now for you to engage with your trade association. Let me reassure you, the transformational shift in these organizations is happening in real time. The evolution started at the end of the great recession, and a tectonic shift took place as a result of COVID-19. Leading-edge trade associations are jumping on the bandwagon, and they are positioning their organizations as industry solution providers. Member-centricity is now more than ever their passion and their reason for existence. Good trade associations have an almost mystical feel for the industries they represent. Strategic planning, once the purview of corporate boards and strictly an internal exercise, is now being done at an industry level. It includes industry-focused market research to assess business challenges and industry outcomes. Trade association boards heavily engage in planning exercises and chart new courses to support long-term industry outcomes.

The earliest adopters were the Global Cold Chain Alliance, the National Marine Manufacturers Association, and the American

Bakers Association. It was Thom Dammrich who launched the strategic practice of "We Are the Industry" over two decades ago. Later, the Association for Unmanned Vehicles and the American Frozen Food Institute embraced the same rallying cry for their industries.

Strategic Partnership Opportunities for Trade Association Boards and Industry Leaders

There is hope for every industry that decides to stand together, to work together, to strategize together, and to figure out the best hope for moving forward—together. Your industry may be right at the gates of a major breakthrough. It just needs a right nudge. Success is more likely now than ever before because the recipe for building a successful industry-wide strategic partnership by leveraging trade associations has been tested in a diverse set of circumstances. And it works. The ingredients can be changed around a bit; one thing may be substituted for another, but the fundamentals are tried and true.

In some industries, leaders have poured a foundation that fostered cooperation throughout. As a board member, work toward common threads of unanimity, and use actionable market research to identify critical external challenges and outcomes. Collaborate and build strategic plans and scenario plans based upon alignment on values and the outcomes the industry must achieve. Once your industry plan is built, insist upon a solid foundation of honest communication and transparency throughout the partnership and the ecosystem. The way forward is described by my friend Thom Dammrich, who has emphasized time and again, "whatever impacts one part of the industry will inevitably impact every part of the industry." This makes commitment and trust to help the industry succeed even more important.

The industry strategic partnership implementation will function well if you and your fellow board members determine the operational rigor required to support and sustain your industry well into the future. Part of the functionality will be these critical benchmarks to measure the effectiveness of their strategic partner trade association: strategic thinking; business acumen; focus on data and analytics; defined outcomes; effectiveness measures and key performance indicators (KPIs); and constructive governance, leadership, and processes.

Takeaways from the Industry Stories

Let us summarize these five industries and offer a baseline to move forward with your trade association immediately:

1. **Recreational Boating Industry**—The effort has been to unite a once divided and disparate industry into one voice through an ecosystem of strategic partnerships that extends throughout the entire outdoor recreation industry. Through this ecosystem, the industry is recognized by the Bureau of Economic Analysis as a component of the nation's economic activity. The same ecosystem helps to promote recreational boating and achieves greater access for boating and fishing.

2. **Baking Industry**—Through a series of strategic partnerships that extend from the baking industry all the way through the entire food, beverage, and agriculture ecosystem, the industry was united. These partnerships continued to build, and saved the industry millions of dollars from, for example, tray loss in Texas. The industry acknowledges the American Bakers Association (ABA) as its public face, lauds its support of the industry's

workforce challenges, and recognizes ABA's impact in shaping the external business environment.

3. **Unmanned Systems**—Through its strategic partnership with the Association for Unmanned Vehicle Systems International (AUVSI), the unmanned systems community is growing an ecosystem of strategic partnerships (through the value chain) that is helping achieve its primary objective—namely, public acceptance of unmanned systems. This partnership is demonstrating the effective implementation of unmanned systems in public safety applications as part of a long-term effort to win public acceptance. AUVSI is building a series of its own consequential strategic partnerships, notably a mutually beneficial working relationship with the Federal Aviation Administration and commercial collaboration with the logistics industry.

4. **Asphalt Pavement**—Building a committed community together to support and advance the industry through an ecosystem that stretches from every community back to every company in the industry. Operating with science, trust, and transparency, the industry sees the National Asphalt Pavement Association (NAPA) as essential to shaping business strategy now and into the future. Helping the industry achieve meaningful outcomes to protect its workers, it continues to deliver upon its sustainability and safety commitments. Continually building new and different strategic partnerships extends the reach of the industry.

5. **Frozen Foods**—Building support through data and science for the industry one relationship at a time. The American Frozen Food Institute (AFFI) is building an ecosystem to support industry growth all the way to consumers.

Although I shared numerous stories about the effectiveness of the CEOs who lead these trade associations, they all have high-impact staff teams that make the strategic partnerships perform at the highest levels. Thinking and acting as the industry comes from their ability to see challenges and react accordingly from the outside in. They are also fueled by customer-centricity, and it's constantly visible to the industry they serve. That's why, in large part, these five organizations are viewed as the industry.

Strategic Partnership Opportunities for Trade Association Executives and Their Staff Teams

A collaborative survey conducted in April 2020 by Arlington, Virginia-based Potomac Core Association Consulting and Edge Research identified how trade associations were prepared to advance strategic partnerships in the industries they represented in the post-COVID-19 world. The CEOs of 117 associations from an array of industries (including manufacturing, food and beverage, accounting, banking and finance, construction, architecture, education, transportation, energy, utilities, healthcare, real estate, agriculture, forestry, fishing, insurance, and technology) participated in the research.

Asking participants to share their insights from an industry perspective provided valuable opportunities for company executives. Trade association CEOs affirm federal-level advocacy, representation, and legislation as top priorities, and they rate their associations highly on these key metrics. Advocacy remains a key deliverable as industries seek even greater support in shaping the external environment, and many of these organizations plan to increase their capacity to support their industry.

The shift in trade associations at the start of the global pandemic was noteworthy. It confirmed that these organizations now serve as the face of their industries. At the urging of their industries, they expanded their roles including obtaining critical infrastructure and workforce designations all the way to securing personal protective equipment (PPE) to protect their workers. Industry leaders praised these actions, and executives set their sights even higher. With greater industry expectations, our research shows how trade associations are evolving and working to reinforce their industry strategic partnerships through aggressive implementation of the following deliverables:

- Serving as a top resource for information, updates, and trend reports
- Flexibility/nimbleness to meet new challenges
- Raising public awareness and improving public perceptions of the industry
- Expertise on key issue areas and market trends
- Regularly engaging with/taking the pulse of members to understand and center their needs

One of the other important findings by the same trade association executives is also noteworthy. Expanding offerings of a wider variety of training and education resources to support members and industry segments to help increase the skills of the workforce is a more important deliverable than ever.

One participating trade association CEO noted that the disruptive nature of the pandemic forces a redefinition of member and industry value. Moving forward, organizations have opportunities to improve alignment with emerging member and industry expectations.

Essentially, this research opens the door to a new strategic imperative for trade associations and CEOs.

The trade associations reflect in large measure the sentiments shared in the industry case studies. CEOs and their trade associations are advancing capabilities and becoming far more nimble, and they are positioning their organizations to help industries deal with a rapid pace of change and uncertainty.

Two other CEOs who completed the survey magnified the rapid shift. They see their role as a strategic partner employing a more fluid approach to support industries and help them navigate through uncertainty:

"Vision (to help members see what is on the horizon) and flexibility (to be able to adjust to new business conditions very quickly)."

"Nimbleness to take advantage of changing environments quickly."

The industry leader interviews (conducted for the case studies) also provide key insights about essential expectations of their trade association CEOs. Humility, collaboration, the ability to extend the reach of the industry through strategic partnerships through their trade association are viewed as more important nowadays. As industry leaders become even more focused on their business challenges, they expect their CEOs to be the face of the entire industry. From their perspective, it is more important than ever to build relationships that galvanize an industry and help to position it for growth. Having humility, in their view, is an essential ingredient of industry success through the trade association. Long-term success is about the industry and seeing the world through their perspective in a humble manner.

In the movie *Without Limits*, runner Steve Prefontaine debates the importance of his strategy to win races with his coach, Bill Bowerman: "When you set the pace, you control the race." The trade association CEO research, the industry case studies, and the "we are the industry" rallying cry demonstrate that trade associations are poised, willing, off to the races, and ready to utilize strategic partnerships and help industries reimagine industry growth.

Strategic Partnership Call to Action for Industries and Trade Associations

Your call to action is here and your moment is now. The bell rings loudly for industry executives and trade associations. This is the time to reimagine industry growth. For executives who already engage with your trade association, apply the learnings of this book to explore how your industry association could evolve into an essential strategic partner. The door is open, and the opportunities can be limitless if you and the industry move forward together.

For executives who do not yet engage with your trade associations, know that you are missing a key opportunity at a pivotal moment. The stakes are high, and the opportunities are far greater if you engage right away. As global and domestic challenges intensify, strategic partner relationships represent your pathway to reimagine industry growth. Contact board members who serve on the trade association board, share this book, refer to specific case studies, and launch conversations with your organization's CEO about how your industry can engage with them to build your own strategic partnership.

Trade associations can utilize the case studies to brainstorm a way forward. As you observed, the case studies are unique to industries, but the principles are industry-agnostic. Engage your board members in a new and different strategic conversation that breaks away from the current model. Build to a new, more flexible approach that makes your organization and the industry more durable over the long term.

Strategic partnerships between industries and trade associations work. They are something to shout from the highest mountaintops. They are worthy of immediate exploration, and over time they should be implemented or expanded for your industry and trade association.

ACKNOWLEDGMENTS

On my 14th birthday, my sister Andi (Andrea) shared priceless quotes from Winston Churchill. These messages live inside me every day: maintain the courage to continue and never give up. Seven months later Andi's messages met their first test when she and my younger brother Jonathan lost their lives in a tragic car accident. Andi's messages met their second test three years later. When I was 18 years old, the day that I arrived home from my first year away at college, my Dad passed away suddenly.

Throughout these tragic circumstances, my sister's messages provided me with a lasting beacon of faith and hope. They also instilled perseverance and prepared me for the many mistakes I would make and then learn and grow from. There would be numerous challenges, but nothing has come close to the challenge of the global pandemic. COVID-19 struck like an angry lightning bolt, and the whole world experienced it. This time it was painful and unimaginable for everyone. Andi's messages again inspired me to rise above the challenge and embrace an opportunity to bring hope, perseverance, and faith to others. It was time to launch this book. This project is an act of learning and sharing the light of industry and trade association strategic partnerships and how they help reimagine industry growth in an uncertain world. Thank you, Andi.

Our lives are long journeys and the only path to success is with other people. My experiences at the National Association of Manufacturers (NAM) were transformational. Understanding the power of innovation, and how the best workers and managers build the greatest products in the world, remains a constant for me. As NAM president, Jerry Jasinowski connected manufacturing from policy to the plant floor, then to economic growth, and then to community quality of life. He enlisted the board, staff, and manufacturing community in that vision. From it we learned from each other, and we thrived. I was blessed to work with Jerry and talented colleagues Don Sciolaro, Jeff Wansley, Nancy Clancy, Kristin Bodenstadt, Bruce Stebbins, Joni Hodgson, Patty Long, Ladd Biro, Howard Lewis, Judge Morris, Dorothy Coleman, Bob Cunningham, Kimberly Pinter, Neil Trautwein, Meryl Hickman, Bill Gill, Jim Prendergast, Nicole Lamboley, Brian McGuire, and many others. Paul Huard was a near and dear friend, offering multitudes of invaluable guidance and support. I think of him often and the critically important role that he played at the most challenging times. Mike Konstant was also a bright and remarkable professional with great capabilities. He was a joy to work with and an unassuming and gifted colleague. Mike was the consummate team player, making significant contributions, and he had a heart of gold. Mike and Paul were called home way too soon. When I arrived at NAM, former NAM president Sandy Trowbridge and other former colleagues Forest Rettgers and Harry Ganjian gave me guidance that would endure throughout my career. I miss them greatly.

At American Solutions for Winning the Future, Newt Gingrich was an invaluable teacher and mentor. We worked together drafting tax and jobs policies, and we collaborated on meaningful op-ed articles;

we built a nationwide program to support small businesses, and he and I wrote a chapter on small business in one of his best-selling books. He connected essential dots for me on long-term strategy, policy, and economic growth. Working with Newt's wife Callista and Vince Haley reinforced an incredible learning experience.

Brad Hughes was a trusted advisor, friend, and partner at the Association for Corporate Growth. And corporate leaders including Jack Derby, Jim O'Donnell, Bev Landstreet, and David Mead educated me on the strength of capital markets and their essential role in driving growth.

In his poem "A Creed," Edwin Markham embraces the importance of serving others: "There is a destiny which makes us brothers; none goes his way alone. All that we send into the lives of others comes back into our own." This exemplifies the light given to me by my dad, Daniel J. Varroney, DO. He was a family physician who humbly and selflessly thrived by helping, healing, and offering comfort and hope wherever he was. His example is my roadmap of a joyful life serving and giving to others. Thank you, Dad. My two-plus decades of service as a councilman in the Village of Palatine, Illinois, helped honor my dad while I served and gave to others. Helping to improve fire, paramedic, and police response times throughout the community, and making defibrillator equipment more readily available, was all about people, their lives, and physical safety. These were at my dad's core and something he was especially passionate about. Collaborating with staff, my former constituents, and other elected leaders was also immensely rewarding.

It is a joy owning a small business that finds solutions to serve and give to others. Jon Kulok and Gayle Vogel at Edge Research

help Potomac Core clients visualize the power of strategic partnerships for industries and professions. They are impressive and highly
skilled strategic partners; they clarified my thinking for the book, and
Erin Wagner of Edge did an excellent job preparing the case-study
illustrations for the book. In addition, the partnership with Jon and
with David K. Rehr, PhD, Professor and Director, at the Center for
Business Civic Engagement, George Mason University–Schar School
of Policy and Government, helped launch our Strategic Guidance
Lab. Using monthly pulse surveys, we're engaging with 54 of the most
talented association CEOs to advance a future filled with strategic
partnerships.

I have the privilege to share case studies on five of the more
successful strategic partnerships between industries and their trade
associations in this book. There are many more than five strategic
partnerships with equally talented and accomplished CEOs. They also
participate in the strategic guidance lab group that I moderate, and
each, in addition to several others, could have appeared in case stud-
ies: Corey Rosenbusch, president and CEO, The Fertilizer Institute;
Heidi Biggs Brock, president and CEO, American Forest and Paper
Association; Steve Caldeira, president and CEO, Household and
Commercial Products Association; Donna Orem, president, National
Association of Independent Schools; Marc Cadin, CEO, Finseca;
Kevin Burke, president and CEO, Airports Council–North America;
Melissa Hockstad, president and CEO, American Cleaning Institute;
Bob Weidner, president and CEO, Metals Service Center Institute;
and Nancy McLernon, president and CEO, Global Business Alliance.

Much gratitude to Brian Kumnick: his hard work and keen
insights helped to move this book forward from start to conclusion.
The journey on the book started with Anita Sama, and her early

guidance was invaluable. Thanks to other trade association and association CEOs who are stars in their own right. Each helped surface concepts for the book, including Anne Forristall Luke, president and CEO, US Tire Manufacturers Association; Robert Cresanti, former president and CEO, International Franchise Association (now executive director, head of global government relations network at Accenture); Lori Anderson, president and CEO, International Sign Association; David Chavern, president and CEO, News Media Alliance; Thayer Long, president, Association for Print Technologies; Donna Orem, president, National Association of Independent Schools; Jeff Morgan, president and CEO, Club Management Association of America; Julia Hamm, president and CEO, Smart Electric Power Alliance; Francis Creighton, CEO, Consumer Data Association; Dave Rousse, president, INDA Association of the Nonwoven Fabrics Industry; Pete Pantuso, president and CEO, American Bus Association; Rich Gottwald, CEO and president, Compressed Gas Association; Robin Wiener, president, Institute of Scrap Recycling Industries; Glenn Hughes, president and CEO, American Sportfishing Association; Brent McClendon, president and CEO, National Wooden Pallet & Container Association; Matt Rowan, president and CEO, Health Industry Distributors Association; J. C. Scott, president and CEO, Pharmaceutical Care Management Association ; Britt Wood, CEO, National Association of Landscape Professionals; Andy LaVigne, president and CEO, American Seed Trade Association; Kate Offringa, president and CEO, Vinyl Siding Institute; Andy O'Hare, president, Composite Panel Association; Darrell K. Smith, president and CEO, National Waste Recycling Association; Jim Viola, president and CEO, Helicopter Association International; Chris Swonger, president and CEO,

Distilled Spirits Council; Anna Bager, president and CEO, Out of
Home Advertising Association; Joel Dandrea, CEO, Specialized
Carriers & Rigging Association; Chris Laxton, executive director,
AMDA, The Society for Post-Acute and Long-Term Care Medicine;
James Wilkinson, CEO, American College Health Association; and
many others.

Writing a book also requires stamina and strong health of
the body and the mind. Much gratitude to David Kanarek, MD,
Lincoln German, DC at Spine Care of Manassas, and Allen Dunn
and his team at the Prince William Aquatics Center at Colgan
High School for providing a marvelous facility to exercise and think
through the book.

Special recognition to Strategic Partnership's pioneers: Robb
MacKie, President and CEO, American Bakers Association; Thom
Dammrich, president emeritus, National Marine Manufacturers
Association; Brian Wynne, president and CEO, Association for
Unmanned Vehicles; Audrey Copeland, president and CEO, National
Asphalt Pavement Association; and Alison Bodor, president and
CEO, American Frozen Food Institute. Each of these CEOs and
their impressive and dynamic teams makes a real difference for the
industries they serve. Each of them and their teams were incredibly
supportive and generous in sharing their time and perspectives. The
industry leaders who participated in interviews also provided the clar-
ity that brings strategic partnerships to life in each of the case studies.

Potomac Core is blessed with essential operational strategic part-
nerships that make a difference every day. Susan Daniero and Deven
Cao at Materiell are first-rate web developers and creative designers.
Their web design, SEO capabilities, and professionalism are second to

none and they do great work presenting the company to the marketplace. Tim and Cheryl Singstock at Help Accounting Services are 24/7 efficient, responsive, and consummate professionals.

And to my dearest friends, Ron Kovacs of RadioMaxMusic, Ed Sella of SPC Financial, Donna Serdula of Vision Board Media, Jon Kulok of Edge Research, Robb MacKie of the American Bakers Association, Corey Rosenbusch, the Fertilizer Institute, Kevin Brown, former executive director, CPCU Society, David Rehr, Bill Hudson, Bill Shaffer, and Tom Griffith, thank you for your humor, guidance, and endless reinforcement.

I am blessed with remarkable family support. Anthony Dolce, from the beginning, was a continual source of support; the same for Ray Caldiero. My wife Jeanine, my princess, is the light and love of my life. She is a highly skilled, impressive, bright, and passionate front-line healthcare worker and is my constant inspiration. Jeanine is also the driving force for this book, and she is Potomac Core's strongest cheerleader. Jeanine and our three children, Colleen, Shannon, and Daniel, shine the same light. They serve, give of themselves to others, and they are determined and resilient. Our five grandchildren are also learning about the importance of having this light and serving and giving to others. I love and miss Andi and my dad a lot. Yet I know they're happy because they see all of us walking and sharing the same light of hope, perseverance, faith, and service to others. Yes, it's the same light they shared with me many years ago.

ABOUT THE AUTHOR

Daniel A. Varroney is president and founder of Potomac Core, the northern Virginia strategic consulting firm that specializes in association transformation and building industry and association strategic partnerships. Through his work he engages industry association executives and member chief executives who are recognized leaders in their industry. He also guides association CEOs on overcoming impediments, shaping the challenging external environment, and helping position industries and professions for long-term growth. He has built upon on his own successful career as an association executive, leading groups with diverse focus, from manufacturing to high tech to finance, policy, and advocacy.

He became a sought-after expert on economic performance with appearances on CNBC, Fox, Dow Jones Marketwatch, Bloomberg, and the BBC. His deep understanding of policy, the economy, and regulatory influence on industries has shaped his approach to guiding associations and their boards through a strategic industry engagement process. Through his own management experience—and nearly a decade advising association clients—Dan has successfully applied his unique data-driven strategic process to the business and market challenges of trade groups and the companies they represent.

A prolific blog author, he launched and facilitates a Strategic Guidance Lab group for leading association CEOs with a focus on strategic partnerships and innovation. His unique consulting methodology has grown to include an understanding of the contributing factors of successful trade associations and professional societies, and the corresponding characteristics of the CEOs who lead them.

Dan is also a former elected official, serving as a Village Council Member in Palatine, Illinois. During his 22 years of service, he collaborated with other elected officials, a citizen's advisory council, and staff to reduce police, fire, and paramedic response times, increase commercial revenues, improve Palatine's bond rating to AA+, and stabilize property tax rates.

He graduated from The Catholic University of America with a Bachelor of Arts degree and holds a Certificate in Leadership and Team Effectiveness from the Yale School of Management. He is also a member of the American Society of Association Executives (ASAE). Dan and his wife, Jeanine, live in Manassas, Virginia.

NOTES

Chapter 1: Strategic Partnerships

1. See Ranjay Gulati, Sarah Huffman, and Gary L. Neilson, "The Barista Principle—Starbucks and the Rise of Relational Capital," *Leadership*, Third Quarter 2002, no. 28 (July 17, 2002) (originally published by Booz & Company), https://www.strategy-business.com/article/20534?pg=0 (accessed October 19, 2020).
2. "Fact Sheet: Starbucks and PepsiCo Partnership," *Starbuck's Stories and News*, https://stories.starbucks.com/press/2016/fact-sheet-starbucks-and-pepsico-partnership/ (accessed July 15, 2021).
3. Marty Swant, "The 2020 World's Most Valuable Brands," *Forbes*, https://www.forbes.com/the-worlds-most-valuable-brands/#4e35efb9119c (accessed October 19, 2020).
4. Howard Schultz, *Pour Your Heart Into It: How Starbucks Built a Company One Cup at a Time* (New York: Hyperion, 1997).
5. Matthew Dollinger, "Starbucks, 'The Third Place,' and Creating the Ultimate Customer Experience," *Fast Company*, June 11, 2008, https://www.fastcompany.com/887990/starbucks-third-place-and-creating-ultimate-customer-experience (accessed January 2, 2021).
6. John Pepper (former chairman and CEO of P&G), "What's the Role of Relationships in Business?" (interview), *Yale Insights*, February 26, 2014, https://insights.som.yale.edu/insights/whats-the-role-of-relationships-in-business (accessed October 19, 2020).
7. Jim Collins, "The 10 Greatest CEOs of All Time," *Fortune*, July 21, 2003, https://greatperformersacademy.com/entrepreneurs/10-ceos-that-will-always-be-remembered-as-great-leaders#:~:text=%2010%20CEOs%20That%20Will%20

Always%20Be%20Remembered,the%20underrated%20lawyer%20who%20 actually%20thought...%20More%20 (accessed July 15, 2021).

8. Ibid.

9. Ecclesiastes 4:10 (*New American Standard Bible*).

10. Gulati et al., "The Barista Principle," p. 1.

11. Pepper, *Yale Insights*.

12. Ibid.

13. Public Papers of the Presidents of the United States, Dwight D. Eisenhower, 1957, Containing the Public Messages, Speeches, and Statements of the President, Remarks at the National Defense Executive Reserve Conference, November 14, 1957, p. 817; quote p. 818, published by the Federal Register Division, National Archives and Records Service, General Services Administration, Washington, DC, https://quoteinvestigator.com/2017/11/18/planning/ (accessed 1 March, 2021).

14. Dan Varroney private interviews with Thom Dammrich, April 14, 2020 and June 10, 2021.

15. GoodData press release, "GoodData Announces Strategic Partnership and Investment from Visa," May 20, 2020, https://www.gooddata.com/press-releases/gooddata-announces-strategic-partnership-and-investment-visa (accessed October 19, 2020).

16. Ibid.

17. "The majority of [Americans] believe that a man will be led to do what is just and good by following his own interest rightly understood." Alexis de Tocqueville, *Democracy in America, Volume 1* (Trans. Henry Reeve, Esq.). (London: Longman, Greene, Longman and Roberts, 1862), p. 228.

Chapter 2: Trade Associations

1. Steven Umbrello, "Collegia, Stability and the Vox Populi," *World History Encyclopedia,* August 15, 2015, https://www.worldhistory.org/article/816/collegia-stability-and-the-vox-populi/ (accessed July 14, 2021).

2. Koenraad Verboven, "Roman Associations," *Oxford Classical Dictionary,* https://oxfordre.com/classics/view/10.1093/acrefore/9780199381135. 001.0001/acrefore-9780199381135-e-1695 (accessed July 14, 2021).

3. Jinyu Liu, *Collegia Centonariorum: The Guilds of Textile Dealers in the Roman West* (Boston: Brill, 2009), p. 111.

4. Ibid., p. 113.

5. Ibid., p. 114.

6. *Encyclopedia Britannica*, "Guild," https://www.britannica.com/topic/guild-trade-association (accessed July 14, 2021).

7. *Encyclopedia Britannica*, "Trade Association," https://www.britannica.com/topic/trade-association, accessed July 14, 2021.

8. https://www.carpentershall.org/about-the-company (accessed July 13, 2021).

9. Ibid.

10. Alexis de Tocqueville, *Democracy in America, Volume 2* (Trans. Henry Reeve, Esq.). (London: Longman, Greene, Longman and Roberts, 1862), p. 56.

11. Ibid., p. 56.

12. Ibid.

13. Ibid., p. 57.

14. Ibid., pp. 62–63.

15. https://www.irs.gov/charities-non-profits/other-non-profits/requirements-for-exemption-business-league#:~:text=Trade%20associations%20and%20professional%20associations%20are%20business%20leagues.,all%20commercial%20enterprises%20in%20a%20given%20trade%20community (accessed July 18, 2021).

16. *Internal Revenue Service Data Book, 2020,* "Table 14. Tax-Exempt Organizations, Nonexempt Charitable Trusts, and Nonexempt Split-Interest Trusts, Fiscal Year 2020," p. 30.

17. "GBA Launches Subsidiary for Cyber Supply Chain Threat Mitigation," July 13, 2021, https://globalbusiness.org/pressrelease/gba-launches-subsidiary-for-cyber-supply-chain-threat-mitigation (accessed July 18, 2021).

18. Adam Brandenburger and Barry Nalebuff, "The Rules of Co-opetition," *Harvard Business Review*, January–February 2021, https://hbr.org/2021/01/the-rules-of-co-opetition (accessed July 15, 2021).

19. Ibid.

20. Tocqueville, *Democracy in America*, p. 56.

Chapter 3: Recreational Boating and the Great Outdoors

1. Robert Newsome, "Boating and Economic Impact in California," *NMMA*, October 6, 2020, https://www.marina.org/cpages/economic-impact-of-the-marine-industry-and-boating-in-california (accessed January 9, 2021).

2. "Recreational Boating Vessel Count in the U.S. 2019, by Type," published by David Lange, November 30, 2020, https://www.statista.com/statistics/1156022/us-recreational-boating-vessels/ (accessed January 9, 2021).

3. Newsome, "Boating and Economic Impact."

4. Ibid.

5. Ibid.

6. Rising tide lifts all boats: "The idea that general prosperity is best for individual welfare. John F. Kennedy repeatedly sounded the optimistic note that good times would be beneficial to all. In his June 1963 address in Frankfort, Kennedy said, 'As they say on my own Cape Cod, a rising tide lifts all the boats.'" This reference cites an earlier use of the phrase by President Kennedy in 1960. "In 1993, Theodore C. Sorensen informed the author: 'As Legislative Assistant to Senator John F. Kennedy 1953–1961, I often received material from a regional chamber of commerce-type organization called 'The New England Council.' I was favorably struck by the motto set forth on its letterhead: 'The rising tide lifts all the boats,' and not surprisingly it found its way into J.F.K.'s speeches.'" From William Safire *Safire's New Political Dictionary*. New York: Random House, 1993. Cited at: https://www.phrases.org.uk/bulletin_board/42/messages/1052.html.

7. Editors, "Miami Yacht Show to Change Venues in 2019," *Bluewater Yacht Sales,* February 21, 2018, https://bluewateryachtsales.com/news/miami-yacht-show-to-change-venues-in-2019/ (accessed January 14, 2021).

8. Editors, "New Products, Location Highlight 2016 Miami Show," *Boating Industry*, February 16, 2016, https://boatingindustry.com/top-stories/2016/02/16/new-products-location-highlight-2016-miami-show/ (accessed January 14, 2021).

9. Amy Rae Dadamo, "Texas Marine Officials Report Spike in Watercraft Accidents as Boating Industry Booms, *Community Impact Newspaper,* October 12, 2020, https://communityimpact.com/austin/lake-travis-westlake/

public-safety/2020/10/12/texas-marine-officials-report-spike-in-watercraft-accidents-as-boating-industry-booms/ (accessed January 9, 2021).

10. Ibid.

11. Ed Killer, "Boat Sales Are Up, But Supply-Chain Issues Means Buyers May Have to Wait for Delivery," *TC Palm* (Treasure Coast Newspapers), 10 September, 2020, https://www.tcpalm.com/story/news/local/florida/2020/09/10/boat-sales-up-but-supply-chain-issues-may-mean-delayed-delivery/5749128002/ (accessed January 9, 2021).

12. Ibid.

13. Outdoor Recreation Roundtable, "About Us," https://recreationroundtable.org/about-us/ (accessed February 8, 2021).

14. Newsome, "Boating and Economic Impact."

15. Bureau of Economic Analysis, https://www.bea.gov/data/special-topics/outdoor-recreation (accessed February 8, 2002).

16. Newsome, "Boating and Economic Impact."

17. "U.S. Boat Sales Reached 13-Year High in 2020, Recreational Boating Boom to Continue through 2021," National Marine Manufacturer's Association Press Release, January 6, 2021, https://www.nmma.org/press/article/23527 (accessed July 16, 2021).

18. Ibid.

19. Ibid.

20. "Thom Dammrich Takes the Helm of CSP Board of Directors," *Boating Industry*, December 17, 2020, https://boatingindustry.com/news/2020/12/17/thom-dammrich-takes-the-helm-of-csp-board-of-directors/ (accessed January 3, 2021).

Chapter 4: Baking

1. PWC 19th annual global CEO survey, 90% of CEO survey participants.

2. Claire Koelsch Sand, "Packaging Solutions for Baked Goods," *Food Technology Magazine*, January 1, 2019, https://www.ift.org/news-and-publications/food-technology-magazine/issues/2019/january/columns/packaging-solutions-for-baked-goods (accessed March 15, 2021).

3. John Dunham & Associates, Inc., "The Baking Industry 2020 Economic Impact Study," October 2020, https://bakersenrichamerica.guerrillaeconomics.net/res/Methodology.pdf (accessed March 26, 2021).

4. https://americanbakers.org/about (accessed March 26, 2021).

5. Dunham, "The Baking Industry 2020 Economic Impact Study."

6. Ibid.

7. https://americanbakers.org/membership/member-list (accessed 28 March, 2021).

8. Katie Juhl, "Grain Chain, Led by ABA, Testifies on Health Benefits of Enriched and Whole Grains," August 11, 2020, https://americanbakers.org/news/grain-chain-led-aba-testifies-health-benefits-enriched-and-whole-grains (accessed March 29, 2021).

9. Ibid.

10. Katie Juhl, "2020–2025 Dietary Guidelines for Americans Recommend Grains at All Life Stages," December 29, 2020, https://americanbakers.org/news/2020-2025-dietary-guidelines-americans-recommend-grains-all-life-stages (accessed March 29, 2021).

11. Ibid.

12. Louis Pasteur, Lecture, University of Lille (December 7, 1854).

13. *Bake to the Future*, #26 The Industry's Future Focus with Fred Penny, December 15, 2020, https://podcasts.google.com/feed/aHR0cHM6Ly9iYWtldG90aGVmdXR1cmUubGic3luLmNvbS9yc3M/episode/ZWE0M2M5ZWMtMWM0Yi00OGU5LWFlYjUtN2UyMTQ1NjE1YjFk?sa=X&ved=0CA0QkfYCahcKEwi4ntm3kdbvAhUAAAAAHQAAAAQAQ (accessed March 29, 2021).

14. https://bimbobakeriesusa.com/about-us (accessed March 29, 2021).

15. *Bake to the Future*, #13 Flexibility and Communication in Times of Crisis with Brad Alexander, May 26, 2020, https://podcasts.google.com/feed/aHR0cHM6Ly9iYWtldG90aGVmdXR1cmUubGic3luLmNvbS9yc3M/episode/OWU0YmQ0NTMtNjJhZC00NDcyLWJkYjctN2YwNDIwNzYyN2I4?sa=X&ved=0CAUQkfYCahcKEwi4ntm3kdbvAhUAAAAAHQAAAAQKg (accessed March 29, 2021).

16. Ibid.

17. Ibid.

18. Ibid.

19. Ibid.

20. Ibid.

21. https://www.thekrogerco.com/about-kroger/our-business/ (accessed March 29, 2021).

22. *Bake to the Future*, #2 Leading with Values at Kroger, March 17, 2020, https://podcasts.google.com/feed/aHR0cHM6Ly9iYWtldG90aGVmdXR1cmUub Glic3luLmNvbS9yc3M/episode/OTU5MWY4NjMtZjAzNC00ODdhLTk3Z DYtOTllOTkwYmU0MGVk?sa=X&ved=0CAUQkfYCahcKEwiglO7ojtHvA hUAAAAAHQAAAAAQCA (accessed March 29, 2021).

23. Ibid.

24. Ibid.

25. "Stellar Performance," *Progressive Grocer*, June 13, 2016, https://progressivegrocer.com/stellar-performance (accessed March 29, 2021).

26. "2016 Top Women In Grocery: Rising Stars," *Progressive Grocer*, June 10, 2016, https://progressivegrocer.com/2016-top-women-grocery-rising-stars (accessed March 29, 2021).

27. *Bake to the Future* #2.

28. Ibid.

29. Ibid.

30. Katie Juhl, "Baking Industry Alliance Joins with the USO to Prepare Transitioning Service Members for Civilian Careers," February 13, 2020, https://americanbakers.org/news/baking-industry-alliance-joins-uso-prepare-transitioning-service-members-civilian-careers (accessed July 17, 2021).

31. Katie Juhl, "American Bakers Association Unveils Frontline Workforce Landscape," December 15, 2020, https://americanbakers.org/news/bakers-unveil-industry-career-path (accessed July 17, 2021).

32. Katie Juhl, "Feeding the Economy: One Year Since Start of COVID-19 Pandemic, Study Reveals Critical Role of Food & Ag Sectors in Feeding the Economy," American Bakers Association, March 23, 2021, https://americanbakers.org/news/feeding-economy-one-year-start-covid-19-pandemic-study-reveals-critical-role-food-ag-sectors (accessed March 29, 2021).

33. Ibid.

34. Ibid.

35. *Bake to the Future #2.*

36. Josh Sosland, "Erin Sharp Lauds A.B.A. Focus," *Baking Business*, April 17, 2019, https://www.bakingbusiness.com/articles/48416-erin-sharp-lauds-aba-focus (accessed March 29, 2021).

Chapter 5: Unmanned Systems

1. Tom McMahon, "Overview of the Unmanned Aircraft Systems Industry," *AUVSI's Economic Report*, https://le.utah.gov/interim/2016/pdf/00002258.pdf (slide 8) (accessed April 18, 2021).

2. Drone, UAV, UAS, RPA or RPAS – Terminology (altigator.com), https://alti-gator.com/en/drone-uav-uas-rpa-or rpas/#:~:text=UAV%20is%20the%20acro-nym%20of%20Unmanned%20Aerial%20Vehicle.,object%20employed%20for%20recreational%20and%20professional%20civilian%20applications (accessed April 18, 2021).

3. Federal Aviation Administration, "Fact Sheet—FAA Aerospace Forecast, Fiscal Years 2020–2040," March 26, 2020.

4. "Global Unmanned Aerial Vehicle System Market 2020 Leading Competitors—Boeing, SAGEM, PARROT, Titan Aerospace," *The Courier*, June 22, 2021, https://www.mccourier.com/global-unmanned-aerial-vehicle-system-market-2020-leading-competitors-boeing-sagem-parrot-titan-aerospace/ (accessed July 18, 2021).

5. MarketsandMarkets, "Agricultural Robots Market Worth $20.6 Billion by 2025," *PR Newswire*, January 9, 2020, https://www.prnewswire.com/news-releases/agricultural-robots-market-worth-20-6-billion-by-2025--exclusive-report-by-marketsandmarkets-300984241.html (accessed July 18, 2021).

6. Ibid.

7. "Global Unmanned Surface Vehicle (USV) Market Was Valued at USD 1,513.0 Million and Is Expected to Reach USD 3,096.0 Million by 2025, Observing a CAGR of 12.5% during 2020–2025," VynZ Research (globenewswire.com), May 11, 2020, https://www.globenewswire.com/

news-release/2020/05/11/2031303/0/en/Global-Unmanned-Surface-Vehicle-USV-Market-was-Valued-at-USD-1-513-0-million-and-is-Expected-to-Reach-USD-3-096-0-million-by-2025-Observing-a-CAGR-of-12-5-during-2020-2025-VynZ-Res.html (accessed April 18, 2021).

8. Colonel Dawn M.K. Zoldi USAF (Ret.), "Unmanned Underwater Vehicles: An Ocean of Possibilities," *Inside Unmanned Systems*, August 27, 2020, https://insideunmannedsystems.com/unmanned-underwater-vehicles-an-ocean-of-possibilities/#:~:text=UUVs%E2%80%94submersible%20unmanned%20vehicles%E2%80%94are%20divided%20into%20two%20categories%3A%20remotely,underwater%20vehicles%20%28ROVs%29%20and%20autonomous%20underwater%20vehicles%20%28AUVs%29 (accessed April 18, 2021).

9. "Global Unmanned Surface Vehicle (USV) Market," VynZ Research.

10. McMahon, "Overview" (slide 2).

11. AUVSI: All Things Unmanned, "2020–2022 Strategic Plan," https://www.auvsi.org/who-we-are/strategic-plan (accessed April 18, 2021).

12. AUVSI, "Key Pillars for the Unmanned Industry to Achieve Assured Autonomy," April 1, 2021, https://www.auvsi.org/industry-news/key-pillars-unmanned-industry-achieve-assured-autonomy (accessed April 16, 2021).

13. Ibid.

14. AUVSI, "2020–2022 Strategic Plan."

15. Rushworth M. Kidder, *Moral Courage, Digital Distrust: Ethics in a Troubled World* (Waltham, MA: Center for Business Ethics), February 7, 2005, http://d2f5upgbvkx8pz.cloudfront.net/sites/default/files/inline-files/kidder-monograph.pdf (accessed July 18, 2021).

16. Chris McGoff, "Quad4: Realm of Your Highest Impact and Highest Risk," TEDx, RockCreekPark, May 13, 2013, https://www.youtube.com/watch?v=mmaHvuxLBR8 (accessed July 18, 2021).

17. Brian Wynne, Welcome speech, XPONENTIAL 2021, April 28, 2021, https://www.youtube.com/watch?v=c_tApELeA8g (accessed June 19, 2021).

18. "Cumulative Unmanned Systems Industry Interviews Top Theme Tally," December 9, 2020.

19. Brian Wynne, Welcome speech.

20. Ibid.

21. Unmanned systems and robotics database (auvsi.org) (accessed June 19, 2020).

Chapter 6: Asphalt Pavement

1.   "The Asphalt Pavement Industry Fast Facts," National Asphalt Pavement Industry, https://www.asphaltpavement.org/uploads/documents/117th_Congress_EducationKitFINAL.pdf (accessed June 29, 2021).

2.   NAPA Fast Facts, https://www.asphaltpavement.org/uploads/documents/NAPA_Fast_Facts_Sept_2020_Final_Version.pdf (accessed June 29, 2021).

3.   Virginia Asphalt Association, "The History of Asphalt," https://vaasphalt.org/the-history-of-asphalt/#:~:text=The%20word%20asphalt%20comes%20from%20the%20Greek%20%E2%80%9Casphaltos%2C%E2%80%9D,asphalt%20on%20the%20island%20of%20Trinidad%2C%20near%20Venezuela (accessed June 29, 2021).

4.   Ibid.

5.   Asphalt Pavements, https://www.driveasphalt.org/about/asphalt-pavements (accessed June 29, 2021).

6.   Jeffrey M. Stupak, "Economic Impact of Infrastructure Investment," *Congressional Research Service* (January 24, 2018): 2/19 (Summary), https://sgp.fas.org/crs/misc/R44896.pdf (accessed July 29, 2021).

7.   Jon A. Epps, "Innovative Asphalt Pavement Technology: Paving the Way for the World's Roadways," *Transportation Research Record* 2673, no. 1 (2019):1–16, p. 2, https://journals.sagepub.com/doi/full/10.1177/0361198118820079 (accessed July 29, 2021).

8.   https://infrastructurereportcard.org/cat-item/roads/ (accessed July 29, 2021).

9.   https://www.constructionequipmentguide.com/napas-first-members-organized-for-a-stronger-voice/5689 (accessed July 29, 2021).

10. "Report and Case Study Highlight Capabilities of Asphalt Pavements to Improve Transportation Infrastructure Resilience," *NAPA News,* Release NAPA press release, April 21, 2021, https://www.asphaltpavement.org/uploads/documents/Press_Releases/04-21-2021_NEWS_Bowers_and_Gu_Resilience_Report.pdf (accessed July 29, 2021).

11. "The Silent Disruptor," *Asphalt Pavement Magazine* 25, no. 3 (May/June 2020): 24.

12. Ibid.

13. https://www.asphaltpavement.org/expertise/sustainability/sustainability-resources (accessed July 29, 2021).

14. Warm Mix Asphalt Technical Working Group Charter, http://www.warmmix-asphalt.org/files/WMATWG_Charter.pdf (accessed July 29, 2021).

15. "Every Day Counts: Innovation for a Nation on the Move," Center for Accelerating Innovation, Federal Highway Administration, https://www.fhwa.dot.gov/innovation/everydaycounts/ (accessed July 29, 2021).

16. "Warm-Mix Asphalt Use Reaches New Heights," NAPA Press Release, January 29, 2014, https://www.asphaltpavement.org/uploads/documents/IS138/IS138-2012-RAP-RAS-WMA-Survey-PR.pdf (accessed June 30, 2021).

17. "Engineering Control Guidelines for Hot Mix Asphalt Pavers," DHHS (NIOSH) Publication Number 97-105, January 1997, https://www.cdc.gov/niosh/docs/97-105/default.html (accessed July 29, 2021).

18. "Best Practice Engineering Control Guidelines to Control Worker Exposure to Respirable Crystalline Silica during Asphalt Pavement Milling," DHHS (NIOSH) Publication Number 2015-105, March 2015, https://www.cdc.gov/niosh/docs/2015-105/ (accessed June 30, 2021).

19. AID-PT Annual Reports/References, https://www.fhwa.dot.gov/pavement/aidpt/.

20. Ibid.

Chapter 7: Frozen Food

1. Alison Richards, "Clarence Birdseye and His Fantastic Frozen Food Machine," *The Salt*, NPR, May 18, 2012, https://www.npr.org/sections/the-salt/2012/05/18/152743718/clarence-birdseye-and-his-fantastic-frozen-food-machine (accessed June 25, 2021).

2. Birdseye, Clarence, *Encyclopedia.com*, https://www.encyclopedia.com/people/science-and-technology/technology-biographies/clarence-birdseye (accessed June 25, 2021).

3. Richards, "Clarence Birdseye."

4. "The missing element, public acceptance, appeared after 1929. In that year the Postum Company, skilled in the distribution of consumer food products, together with the Goldman Sachs Trading Corporation, acquired all patents and assets of Birdseye's company for a reported $22 million ($20 million for the patents and $2 million for the assets). Subsequently, the Postum Company purchased the Goldman Sachs interest and adopted the name General Foods." (Birdseye, Clarence) (accessed July 18, 2021).

5. Allied Market Research report, 2019, https://www.alliedmarketresearch.com/frozen-food-market#:~:text=The%20frozen%20food%20market%20size%20was%20valued%20at,low%20temperature%20and%20used%20over%20a%20long%20period (accessed June 26, 2021).

6. "Frozen Foods Ring Up $57B in Retail Sales: Report," *The Progressive Grocer*, February 20, 2019, https://progressivegrocer.com/frozen-foods-ring-57b-retail-sales-report (accessed July 18, 2021).

7. 2021 "Power of Frozen" Report, American Frozen Food Institute (AFFI) and the Food Marketing Institute (FMI), https://affi.org/insights/retail/ (accessed June 26, 2021).

8. Wayne Martindale and Walter Schiebel, "The Impact of Food Preservation on Food Waste," *British Food Journal*, December 4, 2017, p. 3, https://www.emerald.com/insight/content/doi/10.1108/BFJ-02-2017-0114/full/pdf?title=the-impact-of-food-preservation-on-food-waste (accessed July 16, 2021).

INDEX